ROOTS
IN ROCKY SOIL

A mostly peaceful life interrupted
by moments of something else entirely

by Ray and Rose Thielbar

ELECTRIC
MOON
PUBLISHING

Copyright ©2019 by Ray and Rose Thielbar

©2019 Published through Electric Moon Publishing, LLC
Rooted in Rocky Soil / Ray and Rose Thielbar

Paperback ISBN-13: 978-1-943027-32-3
E-book ISBN-13: 978-1-943027-33-0

Electric Moon Publishing, LLC
P.O. Box 466
Stromsburg, NE 68666
info@emoonpublishing.com

All rights reserved. No part of this publication may be reproduced, distributed, or transmitted in any form or by any means, including photocopying, recording, or other electronic or mechanical methods, without the prior written permission of the publisher, except in the case of brief quotations embodied in critical reviews and certain other noncommercial uses permitted by copyright law. For permission requests, write to the publisher.

Cover and Interior Design by Lyn Rayn / Electric Moon Publishing Creative Services
Cover photo courtesy of iStock.com

Printed in the United States of America

www.emoonpublishing.com

Thank you to everyone who read this book in its early stages. Thanks, Carolynn Olsen, for laughing in all the appropriate places. Thanks, Rebecca Roecker, Linda Solum, Kris Hallberg, Beth Lewis, Carol Stouffer, and Carol Kelly for reading the earliest tedious drafts. We are grateful to Margo and Wendell Larson who helped us to get these stories a little more in sequence. Thank you, Polly and Steve Voiles, fellow writers and wilderness dwellers who seemed to really understand what we were trying to say.

Bless you, Melissa Bikkie Ryan, for sharing your experiences from the point of view of the organ donor family. A special thank you to Pastor Angus and Sue McDonald who were great encouragers and actually drove all the way out to our house in the woods to see if we were still writing! Any awkward sentences and ideas are all ours and in no way reflect on any of these dear people.

Sincerely,
Ray and Rose Thielbar

Dear Reader,

This is the story of a more than sixty-year partnership between Ray, the engineer and me, the poet. It's a wonder that we made it this far together, since we are opposites in many ways. Sometimes, though, I am the engineer, coming up with practical solutions, and he is the poet going off on flights of fancy. It's been an interesting journey.

We begin the story as we discover our dream plot in the woods and then add some background to show what brought us this far. We each tell our story as we remember it and try to make it easier to follow by using different fonts for our different voices. Imagine Ray's soothing deep bass voice as he tells our story from his point of view, and my voice as the feminine one, soft but sometimes full of emotion. I hope you will find some occasions to smile along the way.

Sincerely,
Rose Thielbar

CONTENTS

IF I WERE A TREE

by Rose Thielbar

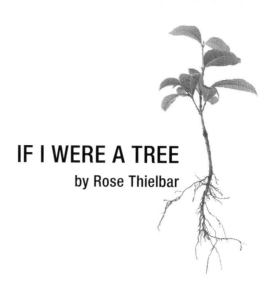

If I were a tree
cut down in the middle,
The rings of my stump
would offer a riddle.

With some rings close together
and some far apart,
Some scars in the bark
and some wounds in the heart.

You would see that some years
I was lacking for rain,
Then you could see others
when I had known pain.

But trees are not humans
and humans aren't trees.
Small-growth years in humans
are the years of ease.

And the years that I struggled
and troubled winds blew,
These were the years
that I strengthened and grew!

THE PLAN

Our budget had very little wiggle room in the early days. We figured that if the car didn't break down too soon, our strength held up, and we didn't lose our health insurance, we could afford to retire early. Then we would build our log cabin and live frugally in the Minnesota Northwoods. We started in central Illinois, and the car didn't break down until we got as far as Superior, Wisconsin. The rest is a long story.

Lake through trees

We drove through the small town of Ely and headed for the woods. Turning off the highway, we followed a narrow lane that wound through conifers and tall aspen trees. Every curve in the road or rise up a hill offered a new glimpse into the forest. I can still see that view in my memory where I fell in love with our

Northwoods property. And we weren't even there yet. The road was lightly traveled, with bare earth and grass growing up in the center. This only added to the appeal. It was almost like we had the whole woods to ourselves.

We were leaving the noisy, busy world behind. Some of the busyness came from trying to conform to other people's ideas of what our lives should be. Some of the noise was the roar of the manufacturing plant where Ray worked to build heavy earth-moving equipment. But even the factory noise couldn't compare to the constant roar of traffic in one of the largest cities in the world. But on this day, in 1981, driving on this narrow, tree-lined road, there were hints that we were about to find the quietness that we were looking for.

We parked near a hundred-year-old log cabin and began the climb from lake level up the hill. We followed a faint animal trail into a lovely stand of red pines. A few majestic white pines with their random boughs rose above the rest of the forest, their needles soft and delicate. Each step toward the top of the ridge gave a new perspective of this beautiful lake. Sun rays filtered through pine branches making shadows on the mossy rocks. Pine needles, a golden brown, carpeted the forest floor, and the scent of earth and trees stirred up feelings of home. It took me back to the days when I walked alone in the woods near my childhood home. But the clear, Minnesota water made it even better.

Small birds and animals rustled in the underbrush, unseen. Somewhere in the distance, the call of a loon echoed through the woods. The air was crisp and invigorating, and the view of the lake from the top of the hillside could have been the dawn of creation. The water and sky were the deep blue of early spring. The lake sparkled where a slight breeze ruffled the surface. I could have stayed in this place forever and gazed at the lake.

It is interesting how a thing like the weather can change the course of your life. Rose and I had decided to spend a week camping and canoeing at Fenske Lake Campground north of Ely. It was late April and we thought surely the ice would be off the lakes by then. Little did we know the length of a northern winter. There was still sufficient ice on the lake to make canoeing difficult, not to mention inadvisable. Since we could not canoe, we decided to check with realtors in the area and look at available properties. After a couple of days looking at run-down cabins, we were thrilled when we saw the property that Rose described above.

Meanwhile, warming temperatures had melted the last of the lake ice, so we brought our canoe from the campsite and paddled around the lake to get a better look at the land from the water.

Viewed from the water, this plot was even more lovely. The water was extraordinarily clear as it lapped at the sides of our canoe. We paddled around the lake and found islands to explore, bays where turtles could sun on logs and an osprey nest reaching

Almost ice out

13

up to the sky. Across the lake, we could see some summer cabins but no other year-round homes.

When the light and shadow were just right, we could see deep below the surface of the water. Paddling was effortless on this calm, spring day. We drifted along the shoreline just trying to soak in all that rugged beauty. The peace was almost a physical entity. I could feel it seep into my soul.

As we rounded the point, we saw a rock crevasse that extended partway up the hill. Cedars clung here and there along the rocky shore with one tree stretching out over the lake. Small ferns had taken hold in fissures on the rock wall. Handily, we found a nice, canoe-sized, flat spot at lake level. We knew it would be a bit of a hike, but we thought it might be a good place to build a future dock.

We came back the next day just to see if this place was as beautiful as we thought it was that first day. The tall pines were still just as splendid, but we began looking at the property more seriously, thinking about where we might build a road to navigate the hill and where we might build a cabin. Walking anywhere but the edge of the property was more difficult. We spotted a tangle of mixed growth where logging had taken out the choice trees. We noticed that when trees blew over, they pulled up shards of ledge rock.

A little prickle of warning skittered up my spine as I wondered how often the wind blew that hard up here on this hillside. Balsams grew so thick that you had to walk around groups of them, and the ground underfoot was rocky and uneven. Still, this was an extraordinary plot of lakeshore property. Thankfully, some of the early loggers had the foresight to leave mature trees at the edges of lakes and roadsides. We spotted two or three possible building sites with a view of the lake, but we would need to clear the tangle of fallen trees first. Uninitiated as we were, we could hardly wait to get started.

Looking out on the lake from a hilltop, I thought we could live here. It was a momentous decision, and I was in the mood to grab the opportunity. This parcel included 750 feet of shoreline on a truly beautiful lake. Our week was nearly spent, so we made an offer on the property, put some earnest money down, and drove home to Illinois.

This was 1981, so we would have been 45 and 43. The kids were in their twenties and well on their way to becoming self-sufficient. We could scarcely believe we were so close to realizing our dream of having a place in the Northwoods.

I started leafing through stacks of log cabin magazines and drew up about eighty variations of floor plans for our future cabin. I hoped to put as much living space as possible into a size that was affordable. The numbers we arrived at were 34 x 26 feet with a three-quarter loft and, hopefully, a basement. Of course, that was before we actually started to dig in this rocky soil. We had just one more hurdle to jump before we could begin our project.

We were on our first home-leave from a five-year assignment with Caterpillar in Brazil. In a few days, we would be on a plane flying back to São Paulo. That plane trip from Peoria took almost twenty-four hours, so we just leaned back in our seats and let our minds revisit some of our memories of growing up in Illinois farm country in the 1940s and '50s.

SECTION 1

YOUNG AND CLUELESS

The early years made us strong enough to get through the years that followed. And the middle years made our desire for peace and quiet more of a necessity. Our journey together began one day when we were in junior high school.

The first time I saw Ray, he was carrying an ornate corner shelf that he had made in shop class. He had wavy dark hair, a deep bass voice, and an attitude of self-confidence. He was one of those "older boys" in the ninth grade. I was waiting on the school bus that delivered those of us who lived on farms to our homes, and I watched as he carried the shelf onto the bus. I remember the shelf because it was unique and detailed with cutouts in the shape of maple leaves. He was a town kid, so I knew he wasn't on our bus route. He walked right past me and presented this unique piece of art to one of my best girlfriends.

I liked Ray because he was everything I was not. He was positive and outgoing, and he was good at building and fixing things. We were opposites in almost every way and for the most part, that was a good thing. At times, Ray's enthusiasm would get the best of him and he would take a notion to start some new project. Sometimes, without much forethought.

Then other times, like when we're telling a story, I would want to get right to the point and he was taking the long way around, including details that had nothing to do with the story. By the time he got back to the story, he might have even missed the punch line. Of course, it was the engineer in Ray that first attracted me to him. That and the dark curl that hung over a very masculine forehead. Then too, there was that sober jaw that suggested integrity. His firm jawline was softened by a slightly crooked mouth on one side which made it look like he was smiling about some secret thought. Aunt Fern said he looked like a movie star. I didn't really see that at the time because I was looking for characteristics that went beyond skin deep. Mom had warned me about guys that were too handsome. Now, sixty-plus years later, looking at old photographs, I can see why he was such a magnet for the ladies. Every time I go somewhere by myself, most of the ladies tell me to "say hi to your husband." Aunt Fern was right. He was movie star handsome and, now, unlike most men who are above a certain age, he still has hair. I am blessed.

Ray also liked to talk on the telephone while I was never so happy as when they invented email. He liked to be working on many projects at once, and the more projects he had going, the happier he was. I was a girl who liked to cross things off my to-do list and I was easily overwhelmed by a calendar that had no empty spaces on it.

FIRST DATE

I started noticing Rose when she was in junior high school. It must have been the way her long, blond hair framed her face, her ready smile that seemed always present and fresh. I loved the sound of her laughter that was authentic, not forced. She was comfortable with who she was and easy to talk with. The details are lost in cyber space, a term not even known at the time. By asking some questions, I found she lived on a farm and raised cattle as a 4-H project. The only sports she participated in that I was aware of at the time were volleyball and archery. Though I did not have the opportunity to watch her play much, I noticed that she was athletic and moved with ease. Walking in the halls at school, my eyes were drawn to her. It seemed like when she walked in, the whole room lit up!

One of the more vivid memories I have is the time I approached her before English class, getting up the courage to get down on one knee and ask if she would go on a double date with me and another couple. I was nervous but relieved when she said "yes."

I owned a 1947 Chrysler Town and Country [Woody] convertible. It was a huge vehicle by today's standards. I could barely afford to put gas in it. After picking up the other couple and making some wrong turns we arrived at the farm where Rose lived. I really wanted to make a good impression on Rose's parents, but the weather was not cooperating. The night was rainy, the roads muddy. Getting out of the car, I heard the distinct sound of escaping air from one of the tires. Oh boy! A flat tire on my first date and poor boy Ray had no spare. Sheepishly, I went to the house, was introduced to her parents and then asked for help. Rose's brother, John, offered to pump up the deflated tire, then we piled in the car and headed for the nearest gas station to have the tire patched.

Thinking all was well, we headed to Toluca to see a movie and parked at a nose-in parking spot. After the movie, we got in the car only to discover the reverse did not work. Applying some ingenuity, I drove the car forward over the curb, down the sidewalk and back on the road heading for home. I couldn't help but remember this night when Rose had to drive down a sidewalk in São Paulo, Brazil, one day years later. But I'll let her tell you about that when we get to that point in the story.

I was frustrated following that first date. Who could have guessed it would rain? Or that a tire would go flat?

Or that the transmission would choose that moment to not engage in Reverse? What would her folks think when they heard the story of our first real date? And what did Rose feel? Upset? Disappointed? Much to my relief, she was still talking with me when we next met. I was impressed with her resiliency and love of adventure, her "make do attitude" when life is less than perfect.

People ask me about going out with Ray after that seemingly disastrous first date. In fact, it was kind of fun driving down the sidewalk in that big, swanky car. However, the introvert in me scooted down in the seat so anybody who happened to be walking by would not recognize me. The side panels of that classic car were made of real wood. That car would've been something to see a decade or so earlier. It wasn't the car, however, that I noticed.

This young man knew what to do when things went wrong. Lord knows, things will go wrong in this life. I could see real potential in him. I was thinking that there wasn't much he couldn't do. And the fact that he was better looking than most of the other young men I knew was only a bonus.

FARM GIRL

The best part of growing up on an Illinois farm was the intimate connection we had to the land. We took care of the land and the land gave back in abundance. Even the woods, which were not a part of the cultivated fields, produced in season. There were wild plums that were so sweet they seem to be a fruit lost to the past. I haven't tasted anything like them since I was a girl. Prickly patches of wild blackberries grew in abundance and were plump and juicy. A few gooseberries could be found here and there among the hills on single bushes. Hickory

Rose with 4-H cow, 1950's

nuts hung from branches of shaggy-barked trees. You could also see walnut, maple, elm, butternut, and sassafras trees.

I loved being a farmer's daughter, and being the eldest child was a privilege. I got to help Dad count cows and walk the fence lines and the flood gap at the creek after heavy rains. Working with cattle prepared me to be calm around black bears on those occasions when I happened to meet up with one after we moved to the Northwoods.

I was always happy to help Dad because that freed me from dusting the house or cooking. Cattle grazed in the meadows and meadowlarks warbled their "all is well in my world" greetings. Sometimes, on my walk, I would just stop and listen to the silence, which is not silence at all, but life bursting out all over. I was free to wander our farm and the woods after chores were finished. I loved taking walks by myself and sought out remnants of an old wagon trail. There wasn't much left of the trail except for the stories passed down through generations, like the catamount that was said to have startled a woman carrying water. At the time, I never dreamed that I would someday live in a place where large cats were occasionally still seen in the wild.

My brother, John, and I had our regular chores which included feeding cattle, gathering eggs, and pumping and carrying water. We carried coal, wood, and corn cobs, and one of my jobs was to build a fire in the cook stove every morning. My bedroom was on the main floor, so I was close to the wood cook stove, but in the winter, it was drafty and icy cold when the wind blew across the Illinois plains. Dad stacked bales of straw outside my room to help keep the chill out.

I raised cattle for most of my 4-H projects; that included feeding, training for the leash, and posturing the animal squarely on all four feet, head raised for the judge. Washing and currying was as much a part of the animal's care as pitching manure and spreading clean straw. I helped in the fields, hefted bales of hay onto a moving hayrack, gardened, picked produce and fruit, and cooked for farm workers. I attended the girls 4-H meetings, as well, but these were humdrum compared to the boys club where we got to go on cattle judging trips. Projects for the girls club were more like work and included growing and preserving fruits and vegetables, sewing and ironing clothes, and baking chocolate cream cookies with black walnuts that we harvested from our timber.

A beautiful stand of black walnut trees lined the edge of the ancient floodplain of Crow Creek. We picked the nuts off the ground after they fell. Dad used to dump them in the barnyard and run over them with the tractor until the outer shell came off. Then we had to let them dry and put them in five-gallon buckets. I can picture Mom sitting in front of the wood cook stove, the oven door open, with her feet resting on the door, picking walnuts. This was a winter chore that we all took our turn doing.

The location of our family farm was an interesting site, not your usual flat ground with miles and miles of black dirt. Besides the wonderful rock-free black soil that the area is known for, there were acres of woods and hills and the wandering creek. The tiny town of Wilburn sits in an irregular bowl shape at the bottom of some beautiful tree-filled hills with Crow Creek winding through the valley. When the day was hot and sunny, I liked to walk the old wagon trail, which was bordered with trees. Dad showed me where a natural spring had filled a water trough in earlier days.

We had a farm kitchen large enough for a pull-out table in the middle, and a baker's cupboard with an enamel water bucket and dipper on the west side. The wood cook stove was on the north, alongside a built-in cupboard. A red hand pump could be found at the sink on the east side. Mom placed a bucket under the sink where we kept the daily peelings and food scraps until we carried them out to slop the pigs once a day. Dad had rigged pipes from the cistern, allowing us to pump rainwater into the house. Later, living in the woods, we saved the daily food scraps for the compost heap.

Most of our lives revolved around that big kitchen. We did our homework at the table, sometimes with an oil lamp for illumination. Our telephone hung on the wall in a big, dark box with the ear piece hanging on a lever. When you lifted the earpiece, the lever raised, and you were connected. A live voice would say, "Number, please." Then we would recite the number we wanted to call. Our number was 17M, a far cry from the ten-digit numbers that we have now. We knew the call was for us by the number of rings; for instance, two longs and a short. Several of the neighbors were on the same line, and sometimes the local wives would do what Mom called "rubber-necking" to listen in on private conversations.

Winters seemed to have much more snow in those days. And I don't think it was just because I was shorter then. I can remember one day when Dad and I went outside to check on weather conditions. Snow had drifted at the corner of the yard where a barbed wire fence kept cattle from getting out. The snow-covered fence was completely hidden except for the tops of the fence posts sticking out. We stepped *over* the fence on top of crusted snow. Normally, crawling through a barbed wire fence is a chancy exercise that can result in numerous snags on the back of your jacket.

Our yard held a catalpa tree that John and I loved. It was big enough to climb, and it had beautiful pitcher-shaped flowers that covered the ground when they fell. The cement cover to the cistern made a fun place to sit and play. I can remember the occasional wanderer, or tramp, as they were called then, sitting there and eating a meal that my mother prepared for him. On the other side of the house, we had a tree with a limb that held a rope swing. Our water supply was a well with a pump just north of the swing tree. Patches of iris, tiger lilies, and hollyhocks were scattered about the lawn. A large, bridal wreath grew in the front yard that was just the right size to race around in games of tag or hide and seek.

The yard was fenced on three sides, and the gate to the barnyard had a brick on a chain that acted as a gate-closer. The gate creaked every time it was opened. I always thought it sounded a bit like the high-pitched squawk of a blue jay. A mulberry tree beside the gate provided seasonal fruit for humans and birds, alike. The water tank where the cattle drank sat across the fence inside the barnyard. Often, we would scoop out a handful of water to wash our hands after doing the chores.

We had the seasonal chores of gardening, gathering eggs, and mowing the lawn with a manual, push mower or a scythe. We didn't need any gas. Our sister, Marilyn, was born when I was eleven and John was nine, so our early memories are mostly about the two of us. Now our sister's house is the one we all want to visit for good home cooking, and she has the best parties.

Our chickens laid their eggs all over the farmyard, in the barn, outbuildings, the granary, or one of the cattle stalls. Mom always said it was important to get the eggs when they were still fresh.

I understood that better when I picked up an egg one day from the back of the barn where I hadn't looked for quite a while. The egg exploded all over my shirt and it was the vilest thing I had ever smelled. I had to discard my clothing in the wash shed beside the old wringer washer before I went into the house.

If you wanted to gather eggs when the hen was on the nest, you had to use a bit of a trick. You had to reach under her warm body, avoiding her sharp talons and beak. Sometimes she didn't want to give up the egg, so we had to decide if we were going to let her keep her eggs. If so, we'd have to remember to not collect yesterday's egg tomorrow.

If we were going to have a chicken dinner, my brother and I had to run down the chicken to the sound of much squawking and flapping of wings. Mom would handle the part that involved a tree stump and an ax. Then John and I had to pluck the feathers.

Sometimes I would help Mom carry water to warm in the sun. Our cook stove had a reservoir that also warmed water. And the teakettle, of course, was always on. It seems that most of the things I learned to do on the farm have come in handy in the woods.

Most of the chickens had the habit of going to the henhouse to roost every night. That was a good thing because chasing raccoons out of the henhouse in the middle of the night was another part of taking care of chickens. However, those chickens were usually on high alert and could really raise a ruckus—one that would wake even the soundest sleeper in the family.

We grew corn, soybeans, oats, and alfalfa. Dad planted watermelons and muskmelons in the sandy creek bottom land. During melon season, we used to drop a melon on the ground to break it and then pick up the pieces and eat them. Dad,

John, and I had no trouble finishing off a nice sized watermelon between us.

In late summer, Dad used to load up a hayrack with straw and drive around Wilburn, giving away melons. Wilburn was a one-store town on a single long street. The post office was in the store, and the train depot was around the bend beside the Santa Fe Railroad that ran along the southern border of our property. Ten or twelve houses made up the entire town. All the surrounding area was made up of open farmland where you could see for miles. John and I rode our bicycles down the steep and winding hill to catch the school bus at the store. It was lots more fun to ride down the hill than to pedal back up it at the end of the school day. We ended up with many scraped knees in those days from taking the curve too fast near the bottom of the hill. My brother always rode faster than I did, and I didn't want to be called a sissy, so I had to temper competition with logic.

Mom was also known for her delicious and abundant home cooking. Her homemade noodles were the absolute best. This is probably because the chickens were allowed free range and fed grain, as well. The egg yolks were bright yellow—nothing like the pale eggs we buy in stores today. Her fried chicken was so good you could eat it cold. She took fried chicken and potato salad in her wicker basket on many picnics to places such as the Peoria Zoo, Starved Rock State Park, or to their favorite fishing spots on weekends.

Dad worked many days from early light until after dark during his long life as a farmer. If he didn't come home for lunch, I would take lunch out to him, along with a quart of partially frozen sweet tea. That is a trick I learned so I could enjoy iced tea when I de-tasseled corn in my teens. Dad always took Sunday off for church and some family fun.

The country issued ration books in those war years of the early '40s when the government determined our purchases by the size of our families. Butter, sugar, gas, tires, fuel oil, clothes, and leather shoes were some of the things we were asked to use sparingly because of World War II. I have a vague memory of car horns honking on the day the war was officially over.

Dad used to back our car into its parking spot on a slight hill, so he could jumpstart it by letting it roll down the incline, then suddenly releasing the clutch. I suppose the reason we did that was to spare the battery.

Our milk was fresh from the cow, so it was warm. That must be why I never liked milk, and to this day, I prefer milk in the form of ice cream. I remember making butter by shaking cream in a mason jar until it eventually firmed up. Later, Dad bought a butter churn with a handle that you had to crank.

Dad milked the cows every evening. I would sit in the hay mow, legs dangling beside the ladder, listening to the steady sound of milk squirting into the bucket. Dad taught me how to call the milk cows to come to the barn in the evenings. Calling animals that were that far away required some volume, so we had to hold our mouths just so and let out a long "Whoooooo! Whoooooo boss!" I suppose a long "Moooooo" might have worked just as well. I wonder if I could still do that. There isn't much opportunity to practice that talent, and if I did, some neighbor over the hill might come running to the rescue.

We took daily baths in an enamel wash basin that was barely big enough to put your foot in for the last part of your sponge bath.

There was an order to this process. We filled the pan two-thirds full of cold water, then warmed it with hot water and took it, along with a washcloth and soap, to a secluded spot. A towel was optional. We started washing at the top, making sure to clean behind our ears and on the neck. We rinsed the cloth and then washed the soap off. Next, we washed and rinsed our arms and trunk. If we started to shiver by this time, we could put our shirt back on. We worked our way down to our feet and then we got to submerge one foot at a time. This skill proved to be very useful for canoe camping and backpacking later in our lives, and eventually, living in the woods when the power went out after a storm.

We grew up in the late 1930s, '40s, and mid '50s, so my parents remembered the Great Depression. We spent money very cautiously. We didn't have things that other people thought were necessary and today we take for granted. We all used the same bar of Lifebuoy deodorant soap and before Lifebuoy, there was Mom's homemade lye soap. The only items in our medicine kit were Watkins Petro-Carbo Salve (better known as cow salve), iodine, and Vicks. I did not feel poor. I knew we had cattle and land. And we always had food. Though, looking back, I do wonder about those times when Dad brought in some unusual offerings; like the occasional turtle, opossum, blackbird, and crayfish, as well as the usual gray squirrel and rabbit. If we were still hungry after dinner, we always had homegrown popcorn that we could make.

Having farmed his whole life, Dad had become a collector of Illinois Native American artifacts, arrows, and other items chipped from stone. One day, while he had stopped the tractor to check out some promising stone tailings, he discovered a burial ground.

I can imagine that Wilburn would have been a desirable spot for a village. It contained hills and trees that hid deer and other animals. It also had sandy soil where the burial was and if you would cross the winding creek and climb the hills that surrounded this interesting valley, you'd find excellent growing soil.

Dad called the university and they sent students out to examine the site. They found several interesting things. One skull had an arrow-sized hole in its forehead which had not healed. Another had a similar hole that had healed.

Rose's dad as a young man

Dad built a shelter over the burial and this little museum became a popular destination for Sunday afternoons. He had an extensive collection of arrows, pottery, and stone hatchets. People living in towns nearby loved this little getaway. Visitors had to drive across Crow Creek at a natural crossing where the water was shallow and there was a sort of gravel roadbed. Dad usually had the tractor nearby to aid drivers who strayed too far from the correct path and ended up getting the floor of their car wet or flooding their engine. We eventually restored the burial site to its original condition after scholars had the opportunity to study it.

Most of the things Dad taught us couldn't be learned in books. One of those things was how to behave around livestock. He showed us how to be calm around large animals, never to make sudden moves or noises, and to remember that if we frighten the animals, they could be dangerous.

Dad also taught me to "never give excuses." He expected us to always do our best and to apologize for our mistakes, but to never blame our mistakes on any person or circumstance. He also taught us that we should have good morals, so I asked him what morals were. I thought he was saying "Merle" because we had a neighbor with that name and I wondered if our friend Merle had good morals. Dad smiled and said, "Yes, he does." That was a good enough explanation for me.

One Sunday afternoon, we had set up the old canvas tent and some army cots. After hours of searching for fossils or pretty rocks and floating bark boats down Crow Creek, we were all enjoying a nap in the tent. Suddenly, Mom made some sound of exclamation and woke us all up. I sat up, put my feet on the ground, and found that the creek had risen to the bottom of my army cot and was still rising. Outside the tent, water was everywhere. Our baby sister, Marilyn, was sleeping in a wicker basket, which by this time, was floating.

We all scurried to gather up our stuff and our baby sister and tossed everything in the car, baby included. Dad tried to start the car, but the spark plugs had gotten wet, so he started honking the horn. Our aunt and uncle lived up the hill, nearby. Soon, Uncle Fred came with the tractor and pulled us all to safety. This was the Illinois version of a flash flood. We didn't have any mountains, just a few hills and valleys with miles and miles of flat farmland. Obviously, there was some heavy rain farther north and east of us. The power of water was often evidenced by the erosion of the creek banks after heavy rains. Years later, one of those floods washed out the Wilburn bridge just around the bend from where we were camped.

Rose, Marilyn, and John with Mom in Alaska

Our family enjoyed road trips and camping along the way. In the summer of 1951, Dad and Mom packed our Hudson Hornet and drove us up the Alaska Highway. This car was a bit low to the ground for that trip, but it was roomy inside. Dad had built a box that fit on top of the car to carry our gear. Our tent was a heavy canvas version with wooden posts and beam. We had army cots and blankets, pots and pans, the trusty iron skillet, a camp stove, and a water bucket. Mom even brought along some large, glass canning jars packed with homegrown food. This was before nylon tents, bags, and nesting pans. I don't know how they got all that stuff and three kids in that car. On at least one occasion, Dad told John and me to "get out of the car and hike up that mountain over there." At the time, I thought it was because he trusted our bush-whacking skills that he had taught us—to always be aware of your surroundings, look ahead to a landmark like the tallest tree or a big rock that was different than others, then look behind you to see where you've been and what it looks like going the other way. He expected us to know which way was north and then orient ourselves by the place in which we started. Looking back, I'm thinking my parents probably just needed a break from riding in a car with three fussy kids. Even though that meant sending my brother and me hiking up a mountain. Alone. In grizzly territory.

COUNTRY SCHOOL

In those days, school was a one-room building where children from our farm communities would walk to every morning and home again in the afternoon. When I was in the first grade, there was a large field between our house and Sulfur Springs School. I could have cut across the field but chose not to because that would be trespassing. I noticed that the adults at church were always asking God to forgive their trespasses. Besides, there were three other kids farther down the road who would walk with me the rest of the way. That year, there were only five kids in the whole school. Total.

They must have closed that country school because suddenly, I had to ride a school bus and attend school in the town of Washburn. My first day of town school was a bit of an ordeal. The building looked so huge as I got off the bus, and I had never been in that building. But I was in second grade, so I could read the sign over the entryway. I saw the words "Boy's Entrance" and thought it read "Boy's Interest." Either way, I knew I was not a boy, so I stood there on the sidewalk by myself, tears welling up because I didn't know what to do.

Finally, a brave neighbor lady came up the sidewalk with her kids, took my hand, and we all marched right in that Boy's Interest. Aw, Entrance. Never mind the label! It turned out that there was a door identified as the Girl's Entrance at the rear of the building. It was a new experience for me to learn some people might consider boys and girls unequal. Experiencing a building with so many rooms and students was also new to me. My horizons were expanding.

The school districts were rearranged after that, putting us in another one-room school named Garfield. We had a two-and-a-half-mile walk, one way. Garfield School was much more interesting because we had grades one through twelve all in the same space. It was so tempting to listen to the older kids as they were up in front reading aloud or writing on the blackboard. In one way, it was distracting, and in another way, we absorbed a bit from every age group.

The school building was rectangular-shaped with a large blackboard on the far wall. A wood stove and a stack of firewood took up quite a bit of space at the back of the room. The school contained an entry room on the front with two inner doors, creating a mud room where we hung our coats and left our over-the-shoe black boots with metal buckles. Windows lined the walls on the west and the east sides of the main room.

I believe this would've been about 1948, and in those days, we had safety drills and were required to take cover under our individual desks. It seemed a little strange that we were worried about being bombed in middle America in between a couple of corn fields. Though, I suppose those sturdy oak desks might have offered slight protection in the event of a tornado.

We carried lunch boxes amply packed by Mom. Our staple sandwiches were usually fried eggs, with the occasional bologna or peanut butter and homemade jelly sandwich. Sometimes, the eggs would be boiled, and Mom would include a pinch of salt folded up in a bit of paper from the Sears catalog.

At lunchtime and recess, we got to play outdoor games like Red Rover where two teams would face off and form a line with hands linked. We would call, "Red Rover, Red Rover, send (Jim or Jane or whoever) over." Then the person we called would try to break through the line of the opposing team, aiming for the perceived weakest link. If you couldn't break through, you had to join the stronger team until eventually, all the players were on the same side. If you broke through, you got to choose one of the persons on either side of where the link was broken and add that person to your team. It was rather fun to have kids who were older than me around. We changed schools again when Garfield School closed, and we went to junior high in Lacon, Illinois, and senior high in Varna, Illinois.

Every day after school, John and I would race into the house after the bus dropped us off. We would turn on the big console radio to listen to *The Lone Ranger*. We didn't want to miss the opening theme song, ". . . from out of the past come the thundering hoof beats of the great horse Silver. The Lone Ranger rides again!" The radio announcer would deliver those words to the finale of the "William Tell Overture" playing in the background. We would plop down in front of the radio and stare at the speaker where the sound emerged from behind the cloth cover.

In high school, my favorite subjects were English/Composition and Typing. I never had my mother's beautiful handwriting, so it was important to learn to type and to do it well. Of course, this was before computers, and Wite-out hadn't been invented yet, so every time I made a typo, I had to rip the paper out and start over.

Dad would give us thirty-five cents a day for the cafeteria lunch in those years. The cafeteria was across the street from the high school and a part of the one-street downtown. When I had typing class, I would use twenty-five of those cents to buy typing paper and the other ten cents were just enough to buy an ice cream cone, which would be my lunch for that day. I always hoped that I would be served by Smitty because his ice cream cones were much more generous. I didn't tell my parents that I was using my lunch money to buy typing paper because I didn't think they would have understood. Our family didn't throw something away if 99 percent of it was still good. Paper was so scarce in our house that we used the backs of envelopes to make lists or do some figuring. Later, I washed dishes at the school cafeteria to pay for my lunch, so I got to have lunch and buy typing paper, too! Dad let me keep the thirty-five cents.

My typing skill won me a job teletyping for Caterpillar Tractor Company after high school graduation in 1956. I worked there until after Ray and I were married and our first child was born. Teletyping was the precursor to computers. I typed on a phone line, much like we do e-mail today. This telephone line was one-way communication, so if I made a typo, I had to call someone on the phone to make the correction. I graduated on Friday night and started work at Caterpillar on Monday.

RAY'S EARLY DAYS

Mom told me about the night I was born. Records show that January 1936 was a bitterly cold winter. We lived in a little house at the top of Sparland Hill. The doctor who helped with my delivery had to alternately warm his hands at the old space heater before going in for the delivery, then back to the stove, then back to the delivery. I survived and lived in that home for the first two years of my life.

My parents moved us across the Illinois River to the small town of Lacon, Illinois. Dad worked as a mechanic at the local John Deere dealership and later for the Public Service Company, and finally, for Central Illinois Light Company (CILCO). When I was old enough to hold a wrench, I worked with Dad repairing cars for extra income. His Jack-of-all-trades ability made him comfortable to work on electrical, woodworking, masonry, auto repair, mechanical, and even radios. It exposed me to a variety of experiences and trades.

I remember the occasion, though not the date, when Mom sat on the edge of my bed and began teaching me how to pray. It started with, "Now I lay me down to sleep, I pray thee Lord my soul to keep. If I should die before I wake, I pray thee Lord my soul to take. God bless Momma, Dad and . . ." That is the way I memorized the twenty-third Psalm and the Lord's Prayer.

I think I can safely say that from the age of zero, I was in Sunday school. Mom being Mom, she made sure of it. Dad would deliver us to Sunday school, and then join us for church. Summer Bible school attendance was also a must. We memorized Bible verses from the King James Version. That is the way I remember them to this day.

My first haircut at the barbershop was memorable. Up until this time, Mom would cut my hair. A flight of stairs stretched from the sidewalk to the lower level where the barber chair was located. The barber placed a piece of wood across the arms of the chair and asked me to sit on it. He sprayed some water on my hair and began to cut. I was amazed at how much hair ended up on the floor. He finished the haircut by spraying some smelly stuff on my newly shorn head to keep my hair in place. I think he charged two bits (twenty-five cents).

During tough times, Mom and Dad resorted to repairing clothes and shoes since buying new ones was out of the question. Our pants sported patches on our knees; decades later, the "in thing" is not patching the knees at all. Soles on my shoes separated from the tops of the

Ray with his parents and sister

shoes and they would flop as I walked. Dad would get out the shoe last, a cast iron form in the shape of a human foot, then re-secure the soles or replace them with pieces of leather. One time, he cut replacement soles from the carcass of a worn-out car tire. I had a lot of uncles, so I always had a supply of "hand me down" clothes.

My first roller skates were castoffs from someone. They were the kind that clamped on to a pair of shoes and tightened with a skate key. My first bicycle was used, and I looked forward to the day when I could have a new one. When I was in fifth grade, my aunt passed down her used trombone so I could learn music. The slide did not work smoothly, so on some notes, I had to force the slide into position. That may have been the reason the band director would frown at me.

Both Mom and Dad Thielbar were industrious people and I ended up with a similar mindset. If I wasn't doing chores around the house, I would be with Dad working on cars or building something.

As summer approached with the prospects of not having to attend school, I suspect I was as guilty as anyone of looking out the windows at the sunny warm days and imagining joining with other neighborhood kids to play war or tromp the shores of the Illinois River.

During my early years, I would spend two weeks during the summer staying at the Jury house in Sparland. That was my mother's side of the family. The Jury family had twelve kids as well as a small herd of cows, a few chickens, and a horse. I was the first grandchild, so some of my aunts and uncles weren't much older than me. I enjoyed going with the other kids to round up the cows and herd them into the barn for milking. The farm was located on hilly land that had a ravine, and the cows would gather in the gully to stay cool. I remember hitching a ride up the hill by grabbing the tail of a cow and letting her pull me up.

(Rose, here: I'll bet that was a fast trip up the hill. At our place, if a cow wouldn't move over in the stall, we grabbed her sensitive tail and twisted it. That was a sure-fire way to get her to move.)

To supplement his income that Grandpa Jury earned working in the coal mines, we would deliver milk to customers in town. Fridays were paydays and Grandpa would come home with a sack of groceries, mostly basic staples such as bread and potatoes. Grandma would make butter from cow's milk. Quite often, the kids, including me, had a breakfast that consisted of crumbled bread, milk, and sugar.

At some time in those early years, Dad and I made a motorized scooter. It was nothing more than a 2 x 12-inch plank about four feet long with an old bicycle fork, a simple plank seat, a gas motor, and two wheels. I had great fun riding that thing around the block.

I had an uncle who owned a fishing boat with a five-horsepower outboard motor that he would let me borrow sometimes. The boat was flat-bottomed and quite narrow. One day, while I was out in the boat, I was making a turn and the boat caught a cross wave and turned over. Fortunately, I was wearing an inflatable, WWII vintage lifebelt. I managed to get the boat and motor to shore. The boat was not damaged, but the motor was another story. It required a new crankcase. I don't recall my uncle ever getting upset over the damage, but I decided to build my own boat the following year when I was thirteen.

I think Dad arranged for my first job where I could earn some money. It was at Longman's Drug Store and Soda Fountain. My job was to sweep and mop the floors each Sunday morning before church. About the same time, I got a paper route delivering the *Peoria Tribune* to customers around town. I added a second paper route and then a third. Often, I would enlist the help of one or both of my sisters, Carol and

Julie, to help deliver papers come rain, snow, or shine.

When I was a young boy who didn't yet possess a driver's license, Dad bought a new tractor from the Leader Tractor Company. It had a four-cylinder Hercules motor and a three-point hydraulically operated hitch. Many of the citizens of our small community of Lacon had their own gardens. Dad saw an opportunity to earn extra money by using the tractor to plow gardens. Often, I would sit on the plow and go with him and Butch, my yellow dog who ran alongside us.

I also mowed the cemetery. To carry my mower to the job, I fashioned a platform on the back of the tractor. On one occasion, I was driving to the cemetery with Butch running alongside us. Dad got the notion that Butch was suffering from the heat, so he shaved him to look like a lion with the big ruff of fluffy hair around his neck. So here I was tooling down the street with Butch, who now looked like a lion, when I saw two elderly ladies standing on the sidewalk talking. I gave it no thought until, as I came alongside them, I noticed they both looked up to see Lion Butch heading right for them. One of the women fainted into the arms of the other. Butch and I kept on moving.

After I got my driver's license, I started working at Lacon Hardware, delivering bottled propane, sweeping the floors, and eventually learning how to run the till and make change so I could sell retail goods after school and on Saturdays. When the owner decided to become a dealer of Homelite chainsaws, I would demonstrate the chainsaws by cutting logs in front of the store on Saturdays.

I realized that I would need considerable funds to attend college, so I took a job at the Lacon Woolen Mill working the second shift. My job was to deliver bobbins of the appropriate yarns to the loom operators. Though a repetitive task, it did involve responsibility. The night I delivered the wrong material to a loom, neither I nor the operator caught the mistake until some of the cloth had to be scrapped. Fortunately for my bank account, management allowed me to continue working.

That fall I enrolled at Eureka College. The next year, I transferred to Moody Bible Institute in Chicago.

OUR COURTSHIP, 1950s STYLE

These were the days when your boyfriend was required to come into your house to meet the family. No self-respecting

Rose at Lake Waubesa, Wisconsin

young woman would run out to the car if her date didn't come to the house first. Of course, once my family got to know Ray, they loved him. Especially, my baby sister, "Squeaks," as Ray called her at the time. Years later, Marilyn (Squeaks) admitted that she didn't even remember me until Ray was a part of the family.

Our dates usually involved trips across the Illinois River bridge to youth meetings at the Baptist church. On alternate Sundays, we all met with the Methodist youth group. Entertainment, friendships, Bible study, and food was all wrapped up in a nice evening out together. Go ahead. Make all the "cheap date" remarks you want. Calling someone frugal was a compliment in those days.

Our other outings were to school functions, choir practice, small-town celebrations, boat rides on the Illinois River, and walks in the woods. When Ray attended Eureka College, he would drop me off at home after youth meetings on his way back to school. This was our best chance to talk and get to know each other as we sat in his car gazing through the windshield. We tried to identify shapes in the clouds as they drifted in front of the moon. "There. That looks like a rabbit." Or, "look, it's wearing a funny hat!"

I found it easy to play the imagination game since I was getting to spend time with my best girl. "That one looks like a fly on the windshield," I said. "Oh! It is a fly on the windshield."

On Saturday nights, most of the farmers would pile the whole family into the car and drive to town for the evening. Mom leisurely shopped for groceries and enjoyed the opportunity to chat with other farmers' wives. Meanwhile, Dad walked up and down the street, visiting with neighbors and townspeople. John and I were permitted to attend a movie

Ray on motocycle

on Saturday nights when a new one came out—usually a western with a couple of cartoons and a newsreel of world events thrown in. A piano was located in front of the curtains on the stage. I liked to imagine that it had been there since the days of silent films when someone would play the exciting

47

hero-to-the-rescue mood music as the villain tied the girl to the railroad tracks. They still played the short films that ended with somebody hanging over a cliff, (a cliff-hanger) so that we would want to come back next week to see if the hero would come to the rescue in time.

After the movie, I usually met Ray, who was just getting off work from the hardware store, and we would go to Longman's Soda Fountain for a green river or a vanilla root beer.

I acquired a small motor scooter—a minibike called a Doodlebug. It was pretty much a basket case. That's what they used to call something that had been taken apart and the pieces put in a basket. It did not have a motor. Dad, being a collector of all sorts of odds and ends, provided a used Briggs & Stratton motor. The memories I had of this scooter provoked the idea of designing and constructing minibikes for our sons much later.

This scooter also became the source of another misadventure. Rose and I were in the early stages of teenage love. During the summer months while school was out, she would come into town with her parents and we were able to spend some time together. On the weekend of the annual Old Settler's Festival, I offered to give her a ride on my Doodlebug. Please understand that when I reconstructed the scooter, I did not have the various safety guards that were in place when the scooter was new. Rose was wearing her favorite skirt—a stylish black and brown plaid. She sat behind me on the seat and off we went, at least for a short distance. It was just long enough for her skirt to get wrapped up in the drive belt.

A quick inspection confirmed that this was the end of the ride. We managed to get her skirt loose and must have gone to my house to get a needle and thread so she could fix it. Later, I tried to replace her skirt with something I thought she would like. I humbly offered her a turquoise Southwestern-style corduroy affair that was much more colorful than what she had. I couldn't help noticing that she wore the old mended skirt more than the turquoise one I chose, but she never complained.

She really was the girl for me, so I decided I wanted to go steady with her. I had acquired a silver ring with an Indian head and two tiny turquoise stones, so I presented this to her.

I proudly wore the ring with yarn wrapped around the bottom, so it would fit my finger. To me, going steady meant we would spend a little time together on the weekend, so I was disappointed when he didn't call the next Saturday. I figured his dad had him working on some old car or another fix-it project. But my mom was insulted that Ray hadn't called me that weekend. She almost had me convinced he might not be helping his dad but enjoying a Saturday night without me. So, I took the family car to town to see for myself. I wondered how Ray felt when I tried to give his "going steady ring" back that night, so I recently asked him to write about his feelings from that night.

The following is what he remembers. Sometimes, subtleties just pass right over that beautiful literal-minded head.

One Saturday, I was unable to meet with Rose. Dad and I were digging a cesspool at our house. This was before the town had a sewer system. Cesspools were a common method of dealing with raw sewage when the house had running water and an indoor bathroom. Constructing a cesspool was practical but labor intensive. The location was determined by proximity to the house and a vein of gravel available below the surface of the ground.

Dad had three large steel rims that were about 54 inches in diameter. To start construction, we placed a rim on the ground at the site of the hole. We used a spade to begin removing dirt about 3 to 5 inches larger than the rim. As the hole progressed downward into the gravel, we set 2 x 4-inch boards, 16 feet long, on end around the outside of the rim. We inserted a second and third rim at appropriate depths to keep the dirt and gravel from caving in. Then we set up a tripod over the hole with a spool at the top and a rope running through it before tying the bale of a bucket.

The person digging the hole [that would be me], would shovel dirt and gravel into the bucket which the man on the surface would then pull up. He emptied the contents into a pile. As the hole progressed ever deeper, we'd drive down the wood boards and steel rims before fastening cleats to the boards at equal spacing to secure the rims. When the hole reached the desired depth, we laid bricks in a circle on the inside of the boards. As we stacked the bricks higher, we slowly pulled up the boards and rims. Dirt and gravel fell behind the bricks, producing a stable encasement. As we topped out the hole just below ground level, we'd taper the bricks in like a dome. Finally, we laid a drain pipe from the house below the ground surface, emptying into the upper end of the cesspool.

That evening, I was at the bottom of the cesspool digging away when Rose drove up in her parent's car. She asked Dad if she could talk to me. When I came out of the hole, she was quite upset with me for missing our date. She offered to give my Indian head ring back. I don't remember what I said, but it was sincere and apparently convincing because she left still wearing my ring.

Well, I guess if I was going to choose an engineer for a boyfriend, I was going to have to get used to being stood up for some old car or another project from time to time. On the other hand, if we got married and lived in some remote location, this was a man who could build us a house and invent whatever we needed.

My first car was a very used black 1937 Ford with a 60 HP V8 motor but no transmission. I paid twenty-five dollars to the local junk dealer for the car and another twenty-five dollars for a used transmission. Dad and I spent many happy hours reconditioning the car.

My second car was a 1947 Chrysler Town and Country wood-paneled convertible that I took on our first date.

My third car was a seedy 1940 Ford, acquired from a farmer who had children. From the smell that emanated from the back seat, they must have been very young children. I spent hours trying to disinfect and deodorize the interior. The other problem with this car was its sluggish response when I stepped on the accelerator to pass another vehicle or climb a hill. I left this car with Rose while I was attending Moody Bible Institute. Often, she would send letters that would include a comment about the car's performance or lack thereof. Sometimes, she'd describe how the car would quit running on her way home from a youth meeting. She would walk to the nearest farmhouse to call her dad or mine. One night, she discovered that the nearest house did not have a phone, so she simply waited for her dad to come looking for her. Which he did. One of our dads would have to fix the fuel line by blowing into the open end to dislodge whatever the obstruction was, then replace the line.

I could always count on my dad. On the night mentioned above, he came looking for me when I didn't get home by the expected time. He found the old Ford at the side of the country road and saw the lights at the farmhouse around the corner. So, he calmly drove over there and picked me up. No questions. No recriminations. No big deal. Thank you, Dad.

Rose included an interesting note in one of her letters that described her exasperation while driving up a hill behind a large grain truck. The farmer stuck his hand out the window motioning Rose to pass him. She tried but the car did not have the power to respond. Rose threw up her hands in frustration to let the farmer know she was unable to comply. That must have been the last straw for her when it came to that car because I heard that my dad finally removed the gas tank and found it half full of soybeans. We could only guess that the former owner's children had put the soybeans in the gas tank. With the car's improved performance, Dad and Rose decided to repaint the car, changing the color from a faded blue to a spiffy black. I took the train home from Moody School to the station in Chillicothe where my family and Rose met me. They let me walk past the newly painted car and laughed when I didn't recognize it. That was a huge surprise.

I was so pleased that Ray's dad trusted me to use the spray gun to help paint the car. Julie and Carol (Ray's sisters) and I covered the windows with newsprint and sealed the edges with masking tape. I got to know Dad Thielbar rather well because of that old car and he remained my faithful ally for the rest of his life.

My move from Eureka College to Moody Bible Institute was evidence that I had no idea what I wanted to do with my life or what the Lord wanted me to do. I took general courses at Eureka, plus a course in geology. As I progressed through the first year, I began to think about going into the ministry. When I was young, I'd been involved in youth work and had some leadership experience at church. In the fall of 1955, I enrolled at Moody. I worked in the Colportage Library to earn some money but began to feel this was not where God was telling me that I should be. Maybe the ministry was not my calling.

I talked with Mom and Dad. Dad suggested I apply for one of the apprentice courses at Caterpillar in East Peoria. I applied and got hired right away in the four-year machinist apprentice course. Including three years of layoffs, it took me seven years to complete the four-year course, plus a year in advanced studies in the metallurgical field. I graduated as a heat treat engineer.

OUR WEDDING

Ray and I were both working at Caterpillar, so we had some income and I had a savings account. My savings account was amassed from the ten cents a quart I was paid for picking strawberries. I did notice that saving the money from the sale of my 4-H cows added a lot more to my balance than the berry money. However, we had experienced enough of the Great Depression to know we didn't want to spend much money on a ceremony that would be over in a couple hours. Looking back from the perspective of many years, I can see now that being too practical just takes some of the fun out of a thing. I was going to have to learn how to celebrate life, but that was going to take some time and a great deal of living.

Our wedding

We tried to keep our wedding a simple Friday evening event since we both had jobs to return to on Monday. However, as you can see from the first photo, the old church was full. I bought a dress that was on sale and Mom ordered a bouquet for me to carry and a corsage for herself and the mother of the groom. We splurged on a three-tiered wedding cake. We hired the man who took pictures for our small-town newspaper to snap four photos. Ray's white jacket came with matching pants, so that is what he wore. That was it! The whole kit and caboodle! We were both firstborns, so we probably hadn't even been to a wedding at that point. Ray was not quite twenty-one and I was not quite nineteen. God have mercy! Please!

We both took Friday off, and I planned to pamper myself with some extra grooming, like doing my nails, for instance. I thought I was going to have the day to leisurely prepare for our wedding and contemplate being married to the talented,

good-looking young man of my dreams. I could embrace my femininity, for a change. Maybe, just for one day, I could be a princess bride instead of a tomboy. But contrary to the popular tradition of not seeing the bride before the wedding, Ray showed up at my house with

Ray and Rose, just a couple of kids (cutting cake)

his sisters, and they told me that we would be spending the day cleaning the church. This small disappointment shows just how unprepared I was for marriage. I felt like someone had shoved my boat out to sea without paddles. Or instructions.

Mom bought cans of Hawaiian Punch and I thought we should spike it with 7UP, but our mothers shot down that notion as a rash idea. The tables in the fellowship hall were laden with gifts from family members and neighbors—all of whom were very generous. We're still using some of those wedding gifts nearly sixty-two years later. These household items and the furniture that my dad found for us at farm auctions were almost all we needed. We bought a new bed, a dresser, and a used TV.

Ray's youngest sister, Julie, who was fifteen, was our talented pianist. In addition to playing "The Wedding March," and accompanying the soloist on "Oh Promise Me," she added a surprise at the end. When it was time for us to march down the aisle as husband and wife, Julie played a stirring rendition of the hymn "The Fight is On, Oh Christian Soldiers."

THOSE UNSTOPPABLE THIELBARS

An older family friend once told my husband, "You Thielbars can do anything!" While not absolute, there are maybe a few granules of truth in that statement. When we were young, we thought we could "do anything." If something broke, Ray fixed it. If we wanted something and couldn't afford to buy it, we tried to make it or simply make do. A directional light fixture in the ceiling comes to mind. Ray made that from a coffee can and black spray paint. The Camp Kitchen that he invented for some of the more primitive campsites we favored was another interesting and useful project.

Ray inherited this ability from a father who was an electrician by trade and an inventor by inclination. If it could be broken, those two men could probably fix it. His mother had an indomitable spirit. In my mind's eye, I can see her driving a bulldozer through her incredibly busy life, singing at the top of her voice. She was a force to be reckoned with. Combine these traits of Ray's father with the unstoppable vigor of his mother and you get the man who became my husband.

I, of course, am not one of those unstoppable Thielbars by birth, but I bring to our union the Braun stubbornness. What I lack in knowledge and aptitude, I make up for in persistence and imagination. I get that from Dad Braun who did things like moving small buildings or constructing a footbridge across a pond out of a discarded hay elevator. As a farmer, he operated heavy duty farm equipment like tractors, plows, corn pickers, mowers, hay bailers, etc. But he was equally as comfortable handling cattle, birthing calves, or whatever difficulty presented itself.

On March 12, 1956, I was hired at Caterpillar as a four-year machinist apprentice. That was back in the days when a job at a large manufacturing plant like Caterpillar could mean a lifetime career. Feeling confident that I had a job for life, and being very much in love with Rose, my high school sweetheart, we got married. That was January 25, 1957. A year later, I was laid off. I was too proud to sign up for unemployment, so I began my own business repairing whatever came my way. Being the son of a dad who could repair just about anything gave me confidence that I could do the same. Occasionally, I'd come across something I couldn't tackle, but I handled enough things well to build a good reputation. My failures were good teachers. During those difficult days, Rose learned how to stretch a pound of hamburger. She also grew vegetables in her garden. She was amazing. Still is.

Slowly, by word of mouth mostly, business began to grow. About the same time, so did our family. Rose made a budget. We determined that if I could earn $16 dollars a day, we could barely survive. We also determined that a business name might be beneficial. Rose, in her always ready support, embroidered Ray's Repair Service on two of my work shirts. That made it official. The business brought in plenty of work but not so much in the way of funds. Rose and I didn't want to charge amounts that we wouldn't have been willing to pay ourselves, so that kept our prices rather low. We managed to keep food on the table and keep the creditors satisfied. We were building memories. Hoo-ha!

I was laid off twice at Caterpillar for a total of three years. Ray's Repair Service became my "fallback" job, even after I had returned to work full time. When I did get recalled after the second layoff, Ray's Repair Service customers continued to call. It was hard to shut down the business.

Ray's career as a heat treat technician started with a four-year apprenticeship at Caterpillar, but his preparation for all of that came from growing up a Thielbar. Ray, Sr. was tall with dark hair and a quiet, comfortable disposition. If he didn't know how to do something, he invented it. Two of Ray's favorite stories about his dad are his invention of the Chicken-Plucker he made with strips of garden hose, or the Ice Boat he propelled with a large, round saw blade. A saw-blade! On ice! Can you imagine what would happen if you drove in a circle with a saw blade as a propeller? I couldn't believe that my father-in-law would let his grandkids ride that thing on the frozen backwaters of the Illinois River. Of course, they had to stay away from the channel, which seldom freezes. I can handle a few calculated risks, but that one was just too much!

I worked at Caterpillar after graduating from high school, starting as a file clerk and working my way up to the traffic desk (the traffic was sales orders) and then as a Teletypist. I was working there when we got married and had to get up at 4:00 a.m. to catch the bus to travel the thirty-six miles to work. Eventually, I found another ride, so I didn't have to get up quite that early. I worked at Caterpillar until our first child was born. It was a pretty short career of less than two years since Bruce came along just a week before our first anniversary.

Betty, Ray's mother, was the most energetic woman I ever knew, and this was a source of competition and angst all the years we lived on the same block as his parents. If it was a matter of endurance, as well as experience, she would win, hands down. I did worry about the high expectations she placed on her son. We didn't know about the effects of continued stress back then. Being a super energetic person herself, she tended to have high expectations of everyone else.

Ray and his mom

Ray's mom was the firstborn of twelve children; all were big personalities, and most were musical. Family visits tended to fall more to the Jury side, which was Ray's mother's relatives. On Christmas Eve we would often end up around the piano with everyone singing parts. We had our own gospel music group we called The Joyfuls. Ray's cousin sang tenor while his wife played the piano; Ray sang bass and I sang the middle part. Later, our kids joined in with musical instruments. I also sang in a women's trio for several years. Ray loves to sing in quartets and has sung both gospel and barbershop styles.

Betty, my mother-in-law, had abundant white hair from the time I first met her. She was always busy with some project. Some days she would interrupt her enthusiastic singing to holler across her side of our huge vegetable garden and announce she had already hoed her half. Our two gardens met in the middle and together, they extended to almost the size of a quarter city block. These were small town blocks, not the big city blocks. Then she would remind me that there was yet another meeting that evening that she knew I would want to attend. I tried to

Ray's mother dunking for apples

make allowances for her authoritarianism since she was the first born of a dozen children which gave her a lot of experience in managing people.

One morning after I got the kids off to school, my mother-in-law brought over a couple of chickens and said she needed me to fry them and make something to go with them at noon for the new pastoral candidate and his family of seven. Seven! She was on her way to take them on a tour of our community. They would be back in a couple of hours. She didn't ask if I was busy or if I had something to go with the chicken. I squashed my true feelings and carried on. Thankfully, the chickens were already plucked. This pastor and his family became some of our best friends. We had kids the same age and our families enjoyed camping and backpacking together. On one of those trips, we hiked twenty miles up a mountain and around the other side in one day.

OUR FIRST HOUSE

Ray adding on to our first house

Our first house, the one we bought when we were newlyweds, was pretty much three sheds attached together with a front porch that had four ornate posts. I remember those posts because a local businessman wanted to buy them. We were saving them to use on the new addition.

The first step was to build a garage on the west side of the house. We took out a loan, but we didn't like to be in debt, so we did the house-building project in stages. Besides, Ray was working full-time and building the house in his spare time.

The second step was to build a large farm kitchen with lots of cupboards and room for a pull-out table and a wood-burning fireplace. We tore off the old kitchen and added the new one between the old house and the new garage.

The third step consisted of adding a second story over the garage for bedrooms, but first, we had to move the garage wall out an additional ten feet. Ray and I did that together one day with his dad's moving dolly. I held the wall up while he nailed it down. We had to work quickly since we were living in the house while the construction was going on. After we removed the roof one day, two neighbor ladies walked by and thought a tornado must have passed through.

Rose and I used a two-wheeled moving dolly to extend the wall out another ten feet. This wall was twenty-six feet long by eight feet high. I made two A-frame supports and installed them at each end of the wall to keep it vertical. With the lip of the dolly under the center of the wall and Rose helping to push the dolly, we managed to get the job done. We may have had smug looks on our faces for having accomplished this feat by ourselves. It proves the truth once again, especially now that we are considerably older, that Rose and I are a team, accomplishing greater tasks together than we ever could separately.

In the last stage, we tore off the front of the old house and added a living room with plenty of space for a piano, bookshelves and a big, round study/game table. We used the ornate posts we had saved from the old house on the new front porch. At the point where the entry to the new living room connected to the kitchen, we had stapled a sheet of plastic. The plastic kept out the elements during the time between building the foundation, framing the walls, and closing in the roof. We did everything but the roof by ourselves. Ray's dad and Pastor Chuck helped with that. When we poured the cement floor in the basement under the new kitchen, it wasn't setting up as quickly as we had hoped. Ray had to go to work the next day, so I finished troweling the cement during the night. I was still in the basement smoothing cement as the sun came up the next morning. Unfortunately, I didn't notice that the steps had been leveled but the extra cement had not been scraped off. That extra cement is probably still hanging off the edges fifty-some years later.

By the time we were finished, the only part of the old house that was left was the ornate porch posts and a few antique bricks we saved for an entryway. We were within walking distance of the post office and the grocery store and at the time, there was an open field across the street. I used to walk home from the store with a sack of groceries in one arm, baby Chris in the other arm, and Bruce holding on to one finger.

Our first house after rennovation

The location was great in many ways and not so great in others. One of the good things about the location was that Ray's parents were just across the backyard. One of the negative things about the location was that Ray's parents were just across the backyard. When we needed to borrow a tool or needed a helping hand, help was just a few steps away. Of course, that's a two-way street, as they used to say. This corner lot offered zero privacy and we felt like we had no life of our own. We never knew when someone might just walk into our house without knocking. Small town living was certainly different than living on a farm with miles between houses. It didn't take long to realize that I didn't like city life.

THREE KIDS IN FOUR YEARS

Chris, Rose, Becky, and Bruce on a hike

We had three children during the first four years of our marriage. This was not the way we planned it, but it didn't take long to realize that most of life is not the way we plan it. Of course, if we had scheduled the birth of our children, we might not have gotten the great kids that we were given. I can't imagine a world without any one of those remarkable persons that God gave us to enjoy through childhood and beyond.

We had a big yard with a maple tree that was large enough for building a treehouse. I was the only stay-at-home mom on the block, so our yard was often filled with the happy sounds of children. Bruce was our first child, and the morning he was born, I called my doctor's wife and told her I felt like I was having a bit of intestinal distress and asked her what it should feel like.

"That's it," she said.

So, we drove to the hospital, which was about thirty-six miles away. Later, that afternoon, Ray told his mom we had a baby boy and she said, "Oh, you do not!" She couldn't believe we delivered the baby without her. We couldn't do that when Chris was born a year and a half later because we needed a babysitter for Bruce.

Bruce took his first step at eight months of age. I was at work and my mom was there to witness it. He has always been exceptionally good at physical tasks but also has the soul of a musician. He was also good at math. Other pilots tell me Bruce can calculate flight plans in his head. He clearly

Bruce "flying" on his motor scooter

was meant to fly, as can be seen in photos of him as a kid "flying" through the air on his various bikes and motor scooters.

I took a job as a bookkeeper for the local Chevy dealer during one of Ray's layoffs from Caterpillar. I didn't like missing those childhood firsts, so I didn't plan to make a career there, but the job did have its perks. I got to see the unveiling of the new 1959 Chevy Impala with the full tail fin before the rest of the community saw it. And then, Chris came along just a year and a half later, so that was end of that employment stint.

I got to be a stay-at-home mom for most of our kids' growing-up years. I also worked for the Lacon Home Journal, writing news stories, doing the social page, pasting ads, and proofreading for a year or two when the kids were in high school. I typed up news stories on strips of paper that were the exact size of the individual columns. Then we would run the strips through the wax machine, so it would be sticky but not so sticky that we couldn't move it around as we put the paper together. When making ads, we used wax to hold clip art on the ad. One of those days, when I was working there, a middle-aged farmer came in and wanted to place an ad. I had to call on one of the more experienced writers at the paper to help me word it. Basically, the man wanted a wife and was willing to pay for a paragraph in the want ads section.

Even though these were busy years for us, making a living, building our house, helping out at church, keeping a large garden and raising three kids, we had our moments.

We had a precious black and white snapshot of the boys

stripped down to their "tighty whities." They were holding the garden hose and filling a shallow wooden box that Ray had built for mixing cement. The boys were intent on making a wading pool. Their enthusiasm and ingenuity were so much fun to see. I could

Bruce and Chris building a wading pool

see a lot of their father in these boys, plus plenty of their own unique personalities.

One year, Grandma and Grandpa bought a tricycle and a pedal tractor, so the boys could each have a vehicle of their own. One day, Bruce and Chris were riding their trike and tractor and were attempting to pull them up onto a very large flat tree stump that was in the yard. It was several inches off the ground. I watched their struggle and was curious to see what they would do when they got up there.

That's when one of the town's businessmen drove by and hollered out his window, "You shouldn't let those boys do that."

I felt guilty and like a bad mother for about twenty seconds and then I thought, Can't you see how capable they are? Besides, he was probably still peeved that I wouldn't sell him the used porch posts when we tore off the old porch. Either the boys proved to be capable by deciding not to ride off the stump, or more likely, I intervened and showed them how to get down safely. I was usually nearby and young enough to enjoy the things they did. It was important for them to learn their own strengths.

Bruce and Becky on his motor scooter

Giving the kids space to try new things must have made a difference because Bruce became a pilot/flight instructor/airplane mechanic, carpenter, businessman, and a motocross racer, just to name a few things. Then there was the year or two when he was a test pilot for experimental aircraft. But that happened later. Much later. Some of my favorite memories of Bruce are the times he made two glasses of iced tea and invited me to sit down for a mom and son chat. He was a child after my own heart but so much more. I wiped away tears every time I made a glass of iced tea that first summer after he moved away.

Chris worked as an auto body repairman/painter, eventually establishing his own business. This gave him valuable experience for his career as an insurance fraud investigator. He is so good at his job as an investigator because his temperament instills trust.

He has such a calm, friendly, accepting manner that people who hope to trick the insurance company just start to confess and ask, "How can I get out of this?

"Well, let's just see if you have a legitimate claim," he calmly responds.

For fun, Chris goes deep sea fishing, runs marathons and triathlons, and recently has taken up canyoneering and rappelling.

We feel very blessed to have such interesting kids. All those adventure vacations that we took them on may have influenced them, too.

When Becky arrived, our family was complete. It was so much fun to have a girl to dress up and watch as she grew up with two older brothers. We have a snapshot of Bruce zooming through the backyard on his homemade minibike with Becky on behind him, clinging for dear life. The look on their faces says it all.

One day when she was four years old, Becky walked over to the piano and started to play "Jesus Loves Me." I was so impressed that I called the best piano teacher in town and asked if she would teach Becky. The teacher said we had to wait until Becky was six. I think we compromised and started her at five. Watching Ray watch Becky play his favorite hymns is almost as much fun as watching Becky herself. She has so much emotion in those gifted fingers.

A few weeks after Becky started first grade, her teacher called to ask, "Who taught Rebecca to read?"

"Ah, I didn't know she could read," I said.

That afternoon when she got home from school, I asked her who taught her to read and she made a scoffing sound and said,

"Well, the teacher did!" Becky was a quick learner. Or maybe it was all those books I liked to read to the kids. We got a similar call when Becky started college. She took an advanced piano class and the teacher called to ask if we knew how gifted she was. Well, yes, we had noticed that.

Having a daughter becomes even more of a blessing as the years go by. You've heard it said that "a son is a son until he takes a wife, but a daughter is a daughter all of her life." There seems to be some truth in that or maybe it's just that boys and girls are different. When the boys call, they ask how we are.

Becky's first purse

"Fine. How are you?"

"Fine," and then they say, "We just wanted to check in."

When Becky calls in the evening, Ray hands the phone to me, smiles, and heads for his shower early because he knows we might carry on with girl talk for an hour and a half. I may not be much of a talker, but I do love talks with our daughter. Long talks with the boys are highly treasured for their rarity.

Becky was two when President Kennedy was shot on November 22, 1963. I was ironing clothes in front of the TV and remember thinking, The world will never be the same. It was like losing our innocence as a country or maybe waking up to the reality that innocence was already lost. Looking back, it seems like that event was a kind of tipping point for our country.

When the boys reached their early teens, they developed a desire for minibikes. This was the era when dirt bikes were popular and motorcycles with the front wheels mounted on long forks were the fad. I proposed that we build our own versions of minibikes with each boy helping design his choice of bike. The size of each bike would be the same as a Doodlebug scooter, another popular two-wheeled machine at the time.

On a Sunday afternoon, the boys and I sat on the kitchen floor with large sheets of brown wrapping paper to draw out full-scale construction prints. "If it's right on paper, it's right" the boys always said. Bruce wanted a dirt bike design and Chris wanted a scooter patterned after the motorcycles with long front forks. With a welder borrowed from my dad, we set to work building the frames, after we purchased the wheels, sprockets, and chains. We adapted a Briggs & Stratton motor for Chris' bike and a two-man chainsaw motor for Bruce's. Let the fun begin.

Dad passed away at the early age of fifty-nine. The Leader tractor, now showing signs of age, remained in the family. I suggested that we restore the Leader and Chris showed interest in helping. I taught Chris how to use a spray gun to paint the tractor. He even added a white racing stripe down the center of the hood and topped everything off with chrome knobs for the shift and hydraulic levers. My contribution was an Oogah horn.

This tractor was so beautiful that it was the envy of the neighborhood. A few years later, Chris and I refinished his Volkswagen Bug. This was the beginning of a career in the automotive painting business, eventually leading to his becoming a fraud investigator. Oh, the stories he can tell.

THE BRAUN FAMILY FARM

After Ray and I were married, my parents bought a larger house for themselves and for the Braun kids and grandkids to visit as our families continued to grow. This house was located next to Crow Creek in the lovely Wilbern Valley. It was one of those supremely crafted Sears Kit Homes that were built in the early 1900s and still exist today.

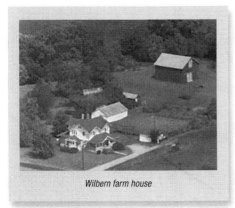
Wilbern farm house

The Santa Fe main railroad was just across the creek. Being near a railroad was almost a prerequisite since that is how the house was delivered. This was a wonderful three-story house with an amazing circular layout on the main floor. You could walk from the kitchen to the dining room to the living room, through the study/bedroom, into the half bath and back out into the kitchen.

Our whole, extended families enjoyed many dinners in that large dining room, exchanging Christmas gifts in the living room and spending many Sunday afternoons on the porch, watching the cousins play together.

Some weekends, we would bring motorcycles and follow trails all over the woods and the edges of fields. Other times, we would bring go-carts and race in a circle out in the pasture, trying to dodge cow patties. We always made time for walks in the hills and valleys or along the creek. Sometimes we would camp out at the farm pond. Dad had built the pond for the cattle to have water available, but mostly we used it as a place to spend time with my brother and sister and their families. Dad had a word for the pond that he learned from the insurance man. The pond was an "attractive nuisance," in that people wanted to go there to play, but it wasn't safe for little kids and if someone got hurt, the owners of the pond could be sued.

It was this attractive nuisance that helped us to name the pond area. We all called it *Camp Hoo Hoo.* The name came about because of the utterance Mom made when one of the grandkids would totter off towards the pond. "Oooh! Oooh!" Mom would shout since the older siblings were off enjoying each other's company and maybe slacking on their watchfulness of the kiddies since Mom was there and seemed to have everything in hand.

Of course, there were plenty of other places to get in trouble growing up in the country. My brother and I did plenty of scary stuff when we were young like crawling through drain pipes under the road. John and I liked to play in the haymow in between stacking hay and doing chores. One day, the two of us stood at the open door of the haymow, holding an umbrella and contemplated jumping onto a pile of "used" straw. I don't remember this part, but I can easily imagine my brother saying, "You go first." We did not make the jump.

Every Easter, my mom made a treasure hunt with handwritten clues, one leading to another and so on. Her treasure notes were fun and incorporated rhymes with hints of where to look

Mom and Dad Braun

for the next note. Mom and Dad hid most of these notes outdoors and it would take us all over the farm until, at last, we found the reward they had hidden. Sometimes, the next clue would be so far away that we had to pile into cars or onto the hayrack, which Dad would pull behind the old yellow tractor. Everybody tried to outdo each other by being the first person to find Mom's note at each point along the way. We continued this into our adult years and most of our kids and grandkids would take part in this adventure.

My favorite thing about Dad was that he was always glad to see me when we came for a visit and would invariably say, "Roselyn, come on. Let's go for a walk." He loved to show me what he had planted and what was coming up in the ground. Dad had the loveliest pale blue eyes that exuded kindness and enjoyment. This is how I imagine heaven: being welcomed by a loving father and invited to accompany him on a walk to explore something he created.

One time, the weekend family project was to move an empty farm outbuilding across Crow Creek to make into a getaway cabin. I should mention that Crow Creek usually carries a substantial amount of water down to the Illinois River. Thankfully, this Braun determination (some call it stubbornness) is tempered by the sensitivities and poetry from Mom's side. After sixty-six years together, Mom and Dad still liked to argue because they saw life from different points of view. This trait has encouraged my brother and sister and even me—the peace-at-any-price dreamer—to become independent thinkers. Thankfully, real life taught me that some things are worth fighting for!

My mother published two books of poetry about her life as a farm wife and mother. She also left her family a handwritten story about her life, living until a few days before her ninety-ninth birthday. I suppose her greatest legacies were her home cooking and her treasure hunts and some pretty good genes. Memories of her bountiful dining room table endure into my 80s. That table featured a bowl of her mashed potatoes, piled way beyond the rim. She would have at least two kinds of meat, usually fried chicken, meatloaf, and a can of her favorite Franco-American spaghetti to which she added hamburger. She also included homegrown vegetables, sweet corn, and the customary bowl of JELL-O. Mom would ask us all to bring our "specialty" to the holiday meals. She usually asked me to bring rhubarb crisp.

The following poems were a bit of a contest between Mom and me. Years earlier, Mom had written an interesting and descriptive poem about being a farmer's wife who wanted to live in town. I decided to write an opposing view about the country girl who lives in the city.

THE FARMER'S BASHFUL WIFE
by Dorothy Jones Braun (early 1940s)

The city ladies can bask in the sun,
While the farm woman's work has just begun.
They can sit by TV and watch Lawrence Welk
But there is Old Jersey, that I have to milk.
But I'm not complaining, for this is my life.
I'm only a farmer's bashful wife.

While ladies in town are out at the wheel,
I'm out picking blackberries on the hill.
They can throw a party for all their friends
And I'm out shelling some corn for the hens.

The girls in town can go to the club,
While I'm washing pickles in the tub.
Some are playing golf out on the greens
While I'm in the garden gathering beans.

Seems the ladies of the city do as they please
But I must pick strawberries on my knees.
Then when evening comes, they are stepping out
And the farmer's wife makes sauerkraut.

Those leisurely ladies can read a book
But the farmer's wife must brew and cook.
They go to the store for a TV meal,
But the farmer's wife has to fry and peel.

They can lie in the sun and tan their legs,
But it's time for me to gather the eggs.
I must can those apples before they spoil,
Yes, a farmer's wife has endless toil.
But I'm not complaining, for this is my life,
I am one lucky girl, a farmer's wife!

THE CITY GIRL
by Roselyn Braun Thielbar
(my response, late '60s)

Raised to love country, but more's the pity,
Fell in love with a man raised in the city.
I dreamed of cornrows and beans and new hay
So, I planted a garden to work in by day.

I thought of the country gals walking the lane.
I just walked on hard sidewalks, O' what a pain!
While music of country from wind, bird, and bee,
I was stuck on the couch with naught but TV.

I dreamed of the freedom to wander at will,
Not a soul to interrupt my climb up the hill,
Could I splash in a puddle or climb up a tree
without someone, somewhere, looking at me?

I dreamed of ducklings, cows, and green grass,
So, I raised me a family, two lads and a lass.
I didn't care about teas and white dresses,
I longed for wind to ruffle my tresses.

I wanted water and sun, warm earth, and tall trees
Not neighbors and folks that I had to please.
"Good morning," "good evening," all proper and prim.
I'd rather have bushes and raspberries to trim.

And wild things for neighbors – so non-intrusive,
Not booming car stereos so loud and abusive.
Glaring street lights at night, how unnatural, absurd!
Where are the stars, the moon, the calling night bird?

I suppose that we've changed some, down through the years,
Learned to think of each other through shared joys and tears.
And now we've been married thirty-seven years plus,
The *me* and the *he* that we were is now *us*.

He has his men's breakfast, his committees, and such.
We attend church together, and with friends keep in touch.
But now we live in the country, amongst the tall trees,
And we go to the city for bread, greens, and cheese.

SECTION
2

TRIPPING ALONG WITH KIDS

Living in northern Minnesota was a dream ever since the first canoe trip we took in the Boundary Waters. That was way back

Our favorite family camping mode

when our kids were still at home and were willing to accompany us on vacations. Every summer vacation, we packed some equipment and our three kids and drove to a national park or wilderness area. We filled personally selected backpacks for each of us that contained only what we were likely to need to survive, then we trudged up a mountain or into the most remote place we could find that we could explore within the two weeks' vacation allotted to us.

One year, when we were tent camping and the kids were little, Bruce had a slight cold and was coughing in the night. I thought, *Oh, no. I had better try to nip this in the bud.* So, I reached for the tube of DEEP HEAT, which is meant for sore muscles. I figured it might work like Vicks VapoRub and relieve some congestion. It can be so dark that you can't see your own hand when you're in a tent out in the wilderness at night. I dug around in our ditty bag and grabbed a tube that was just the right size, then rubbed a generous portion on Bruce's little chest and crawled back in my sleeping bag.

I had not wiped the messy jell off my fingers, so I reached for something to wipe it off. I gave my hands a sniff to see if I had gotten it all and then started to laugh.

"What?" Ray asked.

I had to confess right there in the confined space of the family tent that my hand smelled minty, with no hint of anything liniment-like. I had rubbed mint toothpaste on our son's chest. We were all able to sleep and there was no more coughing.

"How is the cold?" we asked Bruce the next morning.

"I don't know what you rubbed on my chest last night, but it sure worked!" he said. "I feel fine."

One of my favorite family photos was the one where the five of us were lined up in front of a stand of pine trees at the end of a trail out in the mountains of Colorado. Ray was wearing a large green backpack with an aluminum frame. His pack belt

Family backpack trip

buckled at the top of his hip bones to help support some of the weight of the pack. He wore a beat-up western hat and had a camera slung over the pack frame. His handsome face was sporting a week's worth of whiskers and a rather sober expression.

Chris, our middle child has a pack that was nearly as big as he was. There must be an extra sleeping bag at the top of his pack. In the photo, he was wearing a favorite pair of tan pants that I had patched at one knee with one of his honor badges. He is slightly bent under the weight, but he has a big smile on his face.

Bruce seems to be taller than all of us, or maybe he is just standing up straighter. He was wearing a cowboy hat, denim pants and jacket, and a big orange pack. He had a satisfied look on his face and appeared to have miles in him yet.

Bruce, Chris, Rose, and Becky with plastic shelter

Becky's pack didn't even show in the photo because it is low on her back, but you can see her cinch belt and she was in the process of adjusting it. Her expression was the most somber of the bunch, but her long dark ponytails were so cute.

We usually split the food between the five packs. It was Becky's job, since she was the smallest, to carry lunch. That way, all our packs would gradually get a little lighter and Becky would have a near empty pack after lunch.

I am on the far left in the picture, also wearing a pack with the shoulder straps and a cinch belt. Let's just say I look like I've been on an extended hiking trip. I did, however, wear a happy grin of triumph at having successfully completed another challenging trip.

We visited a different national park every summer. One year, our family and Pastor Chuck and Ruth and their family did a day hike twenty miles up and around a mountain in Glacier National Park and down the other side. Another year, we hiked with this family up a trail in Maroon Bells Wilderness Area, Colorado. We took this hike after we had a few other trips under our cinch-belts. Ray describes the first backpack trip we made as a family.

The first backpacking trip we ever took was in Rocky Mountain National Park. We didn't have a tent, but we packed a large piece of plastic to use as a tarp which Chris carried on his pack frame. This was an ungainly thing that was almost as big as he was. The rest of us had our usual packs. Open campfires were not permitted so we had purchased a small Coleman, single-burner stove. Rose had organized each meal in individually sealed plastic bags that she'd labeled by day and meal. "Day #1, Breakfast" "Day #1, Lunch," and so on. Most of the food required the addition of hot water to cook and reconstitute the food to an edible consistency.

Under threat of rain, we made our camp. We tied down the plastic tarp precariously, and we fired up the Coleman stove in preparation for cooking our meal of macaroni and whatever else we had. We started to boil water while five hungry individuals gathered around and watched. You've heard the old, adage, "A watched pot never boils!" Well, it's true. We blamed the altitude and the increasing wind. Finally, whether from tiredness, desperation, or a stroke of brilliance, Rose put the macaroni in the water that would not boil and guess what? Lo and behold, the water began to boil.

Not being a physics major, I chose not to expend energy explaining the phenomenon but thanked the Lord for the blessing of boiling water as we all hunkered down to enjoy a delicious meal just before the wind blew our tarp from its moorings.

Rose, Beth, and Becky backpacking

When carrying forty to fifty-five-pound packs up a mountain trail became more like work than vacation, we started canoeing and found that to be an ideal way to experience wildness without having to carry everything up a mountain. A person can get a decent workout paddling a canoe all day with the occasional portage of canoe and equipment.

Having already seen a good portion of the United States, we were ready to declare the Boundary Waters Canoe Area Wilderness the most beautiful place in the world.

We took a different trip every year. One time we hiked most of the way down the south side of the Grand Canyon trail and back up. We drove down scenic Route 1 in California, visited the magnificent Yosemite Valley and got to see the Half Dome and Bridal Veil Falls. We explored Redwood National Forest where the three kids held hands and tried to reach around one of the giant sequoia trees. They couldn't even reach halfway. We visited Yellowstone National Park and walked on those precarious, wooden planks around steaming geysers. We visited Craters of the Moon National Monument in Idaho one summer. Craters of the Moon was not beautiful in the usual sense, but it was one of the most interesting places we visited. A strong wind blew

Becky, Chris, and Bruce trying to reach around a giant sequoia

volcanic ash into our tent and it sifted into everything. This is where Ray lost his favorite hat that I had thrown away at least once in the past. Unfortunately, the boys were able to rescue it.

We also explored the Great Smoky Mountains and canoed in the Okefenokee Swamp on the Suwannee River. I had wanted to see an alligator living in his natural habitat, so we stopped by a place in Georgia that advertised canoes to rent on the Suwannee River. That was one of the years that we only had Becky with us and her best friend, Beth. We were excited to get to canoe in the Okefenokee Swamp and were only mildly alarmed by the two men who rented the canoes to us. It was the way they looked at us. We sort of felt like we ought to hear banjos playing the theme from the movie *Deliverance* in the background.

Clearly, we didn't know what we were getting into. We put the girls in one canoe and Ray and I took the other one. We paddled leisurely along the river, which was mostly just a marsh winding through trees. As we got a little farther into the bayou, we could see the heads and nostrils of alligators poking up through the water. As we paddled closer, the gators would submerge. I shiver at the thought of that, now. I can't believe we took another person's child, let alone our own daughter, to that place. I can still see the look of horror on Beth's mother's face as we showed slides of our trip.

One year, Ray and I took a canoe trip with my brother, John, and his wife, Val. We left after work one Friday evening after the ladies packed the gear while our husbands were at work. We drove the 645 miles from central Illinois to Minnesota during the night. We arrived at Fall Lake Campground at sunrise and immediately put our canoes in the water, packed them up, and began a ten-day canoe/camping trip. I was hoping for an early stop that first night since it had been a busy week of drying and packaging food. We had driven all night to get there. Brother John had ideas of his own. We paddled past many lovely campsites and were still paddling after dark, searching for some elusive spot that John thought was surely just up ahead. We finally beached our canoes on a rock slab about 10:30 p.m.

While reminiscing about that trip years later, John recalled something I had forgotten. He said the next day, while portaging at noon, I set down the heavy food pack and announced, "I don't know about the rest of you, but I'm stopping for lunch." Knowing when to say "when" becomes important in certain company.

A BEAR IN CAMP

Up until this trip to Oregon, we hadn't had many personal encounters with bears. The time we camped at Crater Lake National Park with its midnight blue water was one of the most memorable. And what we learned there proved useful in later years. If a campground offered a fireside nature talk in the evening, we always attended those. That night, we were taught how important it is to keep a clean camp since there were bears around. After the presentation by the naturalist, we made popcorn at our campsite and were extra careful to pick up every kernel we'd dropped on the ground and deposited them in the fire.

That year, we had a pop-up tent camper trailer we had rigged with three beds on one side for the kids and a bed on the other side for us. We didn't have a kitchen in this camper, which was probably a good thing, as it turned out. Instead, we had a wooden camp kitchen Ray had constructed after I described what I needed. It sat outside the camper. It was about two and a half feet long and just deep enough to hold the iron skillet. Nested pans fit inside. We stored spices and food like Crisco, biscuit mix, and blueberry syrup in the camp kitchen. The front doors had pockets deep enough to store matches and cooking utensils. We kept the rest of the groceries in an ice chest or in boxes in the van. The camp stove fit nicely on the top shelf of the wooden box. It had a top that we could flip open and use as a workplace or table. This kitchen box had holes to insert four legs made from pipes.

On this particular night, we took turns taking baths with fresh, warm water in our plastic wash basin before we settled in for the night. Almost as soon as all the other neighboring campers had quieted down, and the fire had cooled to glowing embers, we heard a loud crash. I raised up in time to see a large bear swatting our heavy camp kitchen, sending it across the campsite. We were all awake by then and watched as the bear sat down and consumed a whole quart of Crisco and tried to remove the cap from the blueberry syrup. When she ran out of food, we started to get nervous. I checked to make sure none of the kids had cookies or marshmallows in their pockets or under their pillows.

Ray loosened the bungee cords at the back of the tent camper, so we could exit if the bear decided to come in the front door. Not that she needed a door. Eventually, she lumbered over to the other campsites, but we didn't get a lot of sleep that night. We had a lot to learn about bears. One of those things was that bears have a really good sense of smell.

When we went out to clean up the mess and see what was left of the wooden camp kitchen, we saw that the aluminum, nested pan set had permanent teeth marks in the lid. We still have that pan set and wouldn't even think of parting with it since it has evidence of our first bear experience. Some families have their good china dishes to pass down, and we have the bear-bitten camp pan set.

CANOEING UP RAPIDS

In the summer of 1975, after months of happy anticipation, we were on the water, enjoying our yearly escape to the Boundary Waters Canoe Area Wilderness.

Canoes ready to go

Sam, our short-legged dog, was a good traveler, and she was very good about not moving from her low spot in the middle of the canoe. On this particular day, Ray was in the stern, keeping us on course. My job was to check the map and deliver some forward momentum. Becky was in the larger, Grumman aluminum canoe with Ray and me, the dog at her feet. The Duluth pack, bulging with pots and pans, was behind the middle seat. Chris and Cousin Bobbie were in the lighter canoe and carrying some of the gear.

The open water of Basswood Lake was a little choppy. The wind had free reign but was a good challenge. Soon enough, we arrived at the long portage around Upper Basswood. We rested, admiring the expanse of the falls, before bending to the task of carrying all our equipment down the path. The abundance of ripe blueberries along the way gave us a good excuse to rest and enjoy some of nature's bounty. The sun was warm on our backs and the occasional splash of cool water was refreshing. Later, we stopped at the beautiful Wheelbarrow Falls for lunch and a swim. I broke out the mouthwatering beef jerky that I had made at home, along with some cheese and crackers. Powdered lemonade mixed with pristine lake water quenched

Cousin Bobby, Chris, Sammy dog and Becky in the boundary waters wilderness canoe area

our thirst. Each of us had our own personal stash of gorp made of nuts, dried fruit, cereal and M&Ms. We were enjoying the easy float down-river while staying alert for sounds of the lower falls that were next up on the map. This was one take-out point that we didn't want to miss, since this was where the water plummets over the falls. We portaged around the falls and paddled across the river to the campsite. We staked our tents on the ledge with a clear view of this inspiring waterfall. Ray and I relaxed while the kids fished. That night, we were all lulled to sleep by the refrain of cascading water.

Rose at portage around rapids

The next day, we did some exploring before starting back. We had paddled upstream as far as the long portage and were feeling good. That's when Ray and Chris put their heads together and wondered if they might be able to paddle, rather than carry, the heavy Grumman canoe part-way up-stream. The lowest part of the rapids was relatively mild, so this seemed like a reasonable goal. Becky and I unpacked the gear, so it would be ready to portage and would still be dry just in case they capsized.

With the canoe emptied of packs, it danced nimbly on the ripples of the surface. The sight and sound of the rushing water a little farther upstream did nothing to deter the excitement of the moment. Chris and I shoved off, soon leaving the calmer waters along the shore. As we entered the main channel of the river, we dug our paddles into the water We had no time to talk; all our energy was focused on making headway. We willed our bodies to put out more, and yet more, power.

"Faster! Keep paddling," we said to one another. The force of the water was unrelenting. We laughed at the futility of our efforts but yelled, "Paddle harder!" Paddling up the rapids would have saved some time, but more importantly, we'd avoid portaging the seventy-six-pound canoe for a portion of the 380 rods (1.1875 miles). Our strength began to waver, and we were losing headway. Now, we just had to keep the bow facing the current, so we wouldn't broadside and end up in the drink. We kept our paddles in the water, trying to stay upright while we floated backward until *we could get out of the current. I didn't tell anybody, but I was beginning to feel some pain in my chest.*

I had the movie camera running to record their struggle when suddenly, I noticed that I was panning the camera downstream instead of upstream. I took my right eye off the viewfinder and opened my left eye. That's when it dawned on me that even though the canoe was still upright, they were floating backward,

Sammy dog

despite their best efforts. I set the camera on a dry rock and ran in after the canoe. I could not hold it against the force of the moving water, so Becky came to lend a hand.

By this time, there were four of us floating down the river: two in the canoe and two on the outside, hanging onto the gunnel. That's when the dog decided she didn't want to be left by herself, so she jumped into the fast-moving water with us. Bobbie was the only one left on dry land. He was running downstream to find a spot where the current brought the boat closer to shore. With Bobbie's help, we wrestled the canoe back to solid ground, along with the dog. Then we carried both canoes over the rest of the portage, like we should have done in the first place. That memorable episode of paddling up rapids was a turning point in our lives. It was this lack of strength that awoke us to Ray's need for some medical intervention.

As 1975 began to form its growth ring in my life, I started experiencing brief chest pains as I would go to work. An EKG revealed no abnormalities with my cardiovascular system. My flippant self-diagnosis was heartburn or indigestion, but a favorite aunt, a nurse, recommended I see a cardiologist.

My dad's premature death two years earlier, caused by an aneurism, gave me reason to think perhaps I had inherited the same genetic weakness. A subsequent angiogram revealed that I would need at least three, possibly five bypasses. The cardiologist told us that if I did not have the surgery, I would risk a 50 percent chance of a fatal heart attack within a year. That knocked the old pins out from under us. After the initial shock, we decided to go ahead with the surgery. I had peace about the coming operation. We shared our decision with our family and our church. The prayer support was immediate.

The surgeon had a pair of the biggest, hairiest hands I had ever seen. When I asked him how he intended to get those big paws inside my chest, he said he would just pry me open a bit farther. For me, the growth ring for 1975 would be one of the thickest.

Bypass surgery was still relatively new at that time, so we were sent to Milwaukee. Two slightly older patients had come from as far as Great Falls, Montana, for the same surgery. Their wives and I encouraged each other as our husbands recovered together. The patients had a sense of competition in their recovery, and I could see this was a good thing for all of us. But more importantly, this was a lesson in attitude. Another patient there at the time was extremely negative about everything from the hospital food to having to exercise. Our guys tried to outdo each other in their recovery, and they were the ones who thrived.

Life soon returned to a normal routine with all the things that occupy a growing family. When Ray was laid off from Caterpillar, I worked as a bookkeeper for the local Chevy dealer. And when the kids were in high school, I wrote for the local newspaper.

It must have been during one of Ray's early layoffs from Cat when his dad bought the antiquated, three-story apartment building next door. We would be making payments on the building from the rent that we received from the five rental units. This had been a partnership with Ray's parents. Ray, of course, was to be the repairman and I would do the bookkeeping. While this may have been an ingenious plan, it did have its flaws. It seemed that every time we sat down to supper, one of the renters would hike across the yard with some complaint about a broken water pipe or heating problem. That old building was always in need of repair. Also, not all the tenants were able to keep up their monthly rental payments. This was even more of a problem with the units in which the utilities were included in their fee. Of course, the utility bills continued to arrive whether the renters made their payments or not.

Ray was back at Caterpillar full-time by then and would come home after spending the day as a shop foreman with all the pressure associated with that job. This apartment house endeavor was a lot of work for such a small financial return. These were the days when we, as a society, began to more fully understand the concept of stress. I missed living in the country where I could slip away for a calming walk in the woods. I suppose my need for space was one of the biggest drives to move up north. That, and the hot, humid weather we had in the Illinois River Valley.

As the pages of the calendar tumbled like leaves, the years seemed to fall away more quickly as every year passed. The longer we were there, the more pros we added to our pro-con list, giving us even more reasons to consider a move. We started thinking about how we might achieve a healthier lifestyle if we were to move. Some friends offered to buy the apartment building as a place for their mom to live. They were hoping the property would pay for itself. After we sold the building, we were free to consider the offer of a lifetime.

SECTION
3

Ray and Rose in front of their poinsettia "tree" in Brazil

THROWING MY HAT IN THE RING

Sometimes, opportunities present themselves when you least expect them. In the fall of 1979, I was working as a supervisor in the planning section of metallurgical engineering at Caterpillar in East Peoria, Illinois. In the day-to-day effort to keep abreast of happenings and decisions impacting the plant operations, for which I was responsible, it was easy to get immersed in the status quo. Such was my focus when I received a phone call from the plant manager on a Friday afternoon. He asked if I would be interested in an opening in our São Paulo plant in Brazil. I knew we had a plant there but knew very little about the operation. He said he would give me and my wife the weekend to decide if we wanted to "throw our hat in the ring" for the job. He wanted an answer by Monday.

We spent the weekend doing a cram course on Brazil, the logistics of moving to a foreign country, and learning a second language. We wondered how much of our possessions we could take with us, and what about the kids? Why were we even considering such a thing? On the other hand, we had always enjoyed trying to stretch ourselves. Bruce was on his own and married by this time. Maybe God had plans for us in Brazil? But the company probably wouldn't even choose us, right? Rose thought we should hear what they had to offer. Monday arrived, and I made the call. That afternoon, I was called to a meeting at the world headquarters, located across the river in Peoria. I discovered that my hat was the only one in the ring.

They wanted us in Brazil as soon as possible. We didn't have time for the usual thirty-day concentrated language training; the company would provide an accelerated, brief training, enabling us to at least ask the location of a restroom and some other basic phrases. Rose and Becky got to meet with the Portuguese teacher in Peoria twice a week before I joined them after work. The company told us we would receive a little more language training on the job in Brazil. They scheduled me to fly down for a two-week familiarization at the São Paulo plant.

The next few weeks were a blur of activity, deciding what furniture we would take while still leaving enough at home for the kids. What clothes should we pack? Brazil is hot, isn't it? What appliances would work there? I learned that they don't even have microwave ovens or power lawnmowers. What about passports, insurance, etc.? Becky had agreed to move with us until her eighteenth birthday. Chris and Cousin Kerry would live in our Illinois house. We planned our departure for the first week in January 1980. We left in a snowstorm and arrived in São Paulo still wearing our winter clothes.

BRAZIL YEARS

I tried to get a feel for the place as our plane lowered in altitude. At first, all I could see was miles and miles of nothing but green treetops. As the airplane drew closer to São Paulo and began to circle the airport, it looked like the city had no beginning or end. It was huge. São Paulo is one of the largest cities in the world, and as you descend in an airplane, you cannot see an end to the city. It seems to go on forever into the sunset. Cars, trucks, and buses crowded into multi-lane traffic, all trying to go somewhere in a hurry. High-rise buildings reached into the sky adding to the mass of concrete that was home to millions of people.

It felt like we were walking into an oven when Ray, Becky, and I stepped off the plane. The first thing we did after treading on foreign soil was to take off our winter coats. By the time we reached our destination, nearly an entire day had passed. It was mid-winter in the US and suddenly here we were in Brazil at the height of summer. There were far more people and cars than

I had ever seen in one place before; the air was hot and stale, and the noise of traffic was a never-ending roar. It was time travel and culture shock all in one!

We had already had our first taste of being on our own in a foreign country when we had to change planes in Rio. A voice announced boarding and departures in several foreign languages. We strained to catch when our flight was called. It's one thing to read a number in Portuguese with our teacher in Peoria and something else entirely to hear a stranger pronounce flight numbers in Rio de Janeiro.

Thankfully, one of the local Caterpillar employees met us at the airport and drove us to the hotel. We would have been hopelessly lost in that mass confusion of bumper-to-bumper traffic.

Life in the *Hotel Cá d'Oro'*, (short for house of gold) was one of unaccustomed luxury. We had a suite on the twelfth floor with two bedrooms and a sitting room. We had a refrigerator in our room that someone refilled daily with soft drinks and Toblerone chocolate bars while we were out. Clean towels appeared daily, and someone delivered breakfast to our room. We walked about five blocks to our Portuguese lessons in the mornings, then Becky and I went down to the pool to swim. We sat around the lovely pool area between giant potted palms. Waiters stood by to bring us *cha' gelado* (iced tea) whenever we wanted. The usual drink there was *caipirinha*, a liquor made with mostly lime juice and sugar. I tried it once and it wasn't too bad for an alcoholic drink. Alcohol wasn't "my cup of tea," as they say. They also served strong café (coffee,) *cha matte* tea (very strong tea) from gaucho country, or the national favorite, *cafezinho,* which was very strong coffee served in a tiny cup that contained mostly sugar and cream. The *"inho"* indicates that it is diminished in size. One day, I was ordering a soft drink from Francisco, the waiter we knew by name by this time. I asked if they had Fresca, the lemony soda that I knew from the States. He snickered, so I knew immediately my mistake. Well, technically, it was not a mistake. Fresca is the word for "fresh" and he had no way of knowing we had a soda by that name in the States. I just asked for *cha gelado* after that. Ordering a taxi and trying to tell the driver where we wanted to go was often a challenge. To say we were stretching ourselves was putting it mildly.

When Ray got home from work each day, we had our choice of the formal dining room or the pool level café with a more casual atmosphere. We just gave the waiters our room number and ordered whatever we wanted to eat, and the company paid the bill. The food was exceptional and they catered to American tastes. They offered filet mignon (tender beef), *lombo de porco* (pork tenderloin), and *frango* (chicken) made in a variety of ways. Desserts were usually too sweet for our taste, except for the chocolate mousse. Two other American families were at the hotel while we were there, so we ate dinner at the hotel together or ventured out to some of the other popular restaurants. We also took some weekend sightseeing trips together with these families. When we returned to our rooms after dinner, our bedding had been turned down and there was a wrapped chocolate on the pillows.

Ray went to work by taxi until we could find a car to buy. It took him several tries that first work day to find a driver who knew where Caterpillar, Santo Amaro, was located. We opted to buy one of the American cars with automatic transmission that became available when someone completed his overseas assignment. The automatic transmission was helpful because many of the streets had stoplights at the top of a hill.

We lived in the *Hotel Ca'd'Oro* for three months while looking for a house to rent. I was happy with most of the houses that we were shown but Caterpillar had our safety in mind and did not approve the first few houses. One of the houses was in an area where some of the American missionaries from our church lived. I was interested in that house because we would already know some of the neighbors. The company told us there were too many robberies in the area. Finally, they agreed to let us rent a house that was going to be available when another American couple returned to the States.

Brazil is a large and picturesque country, filled with interesting, beautiful, friendly people and a few who are desperate. Depending on where you looked, you might see waterfalls, strange looking trees, poinsettias growing as shrubs, parrots in the wild, and exotic flowers with a scent too strong to tolerate. And the culture is at least as diverse as the United States.

For the five and a half years we lived in São Paulo, our house was near a very noisy road called The Marginal which runs on each side of the Pinheiros River, also known as the P.U. River by those who were willing to admit their nasal sensitivities. A red, chemical manufacturing haze hovered over our house day and night. We went to sleep to the roar of traffic, noticed it let up for a couple of hours, then it would start in again about 3:00 a.m.

Ray, Becky, and I rented a modest house in *Alto de Pinheiros* (tall pines). The house was made of white, cement blocks

Our house in Brazil before the gated fence was added.

with a fenced-in courtyard and carport. Barbed wire and shards of broken glass on the wall discouraged trespassers. On the north side, there was a garage and a room with a shower attached to the maid's quarters. We were expected to hire an *empregada* (housekeeper) as a sort of financial contribution to the community for the privilege of living and working there. The house came with a small swimming pool and the maid from the previous tenant. Margarita was a great comfort to me when people rang the buzzer at the gate and I needed to communicate. My Portuguese was very basic and also, I was happy to have some help with cleaning.

She didn't speak any English, but we had no trouble communicating. We knew how to say all the important words like *por favor* (please), *obrigada* (thank you), and *con licensa* (excuse me). We also knew the individual words for most everything we would need or use. Making words into a sentence was much more difficult. I was shocked to learn that Portuguese nouns have gender. A table is feminine; cars are masculine. *What?* I think my mouth must have hung open when our teacher told us about inanimate objects having a gender because she cut the lesson short for the day. Caterpillar provided a language teacher for me after we moved into the house. Eunice was a warm and gentle woman, and I enjoyed the afternoons that she came for a Portuguese lesson. She didn't speak English, either.

We all had our share of language blunders. One of the funniest is the one I heard while riding in the back seat of a friend's car with her as we were being driven by her chauffeur. We were happily looking at the sights when my friend exclaimed, "*Oh, bonita cerveja!*"

One of the more elaborate favelas

My friend's chauffeur was silent, but his shoulders were shaking with laughter. What she said was, "Oh, what a pretty beer!" What she meant to say was "Oh, what a pretty church!" *Igreja* (church); *Cerveja* (beer). Easy enough to mix up.

São Paulo was a city of thirteen million people, not counting the ones living under bridges or in the numerous *favelas*. *Favelas* are the shacks that people build from any available scrap of wood or metal they can find to stay out of the rain. It rained almost every day early in the afternoon. Then the sun would come back out. When we finally moved from the hotel to a house, I wrote home to Chris, our son:

"So far, house dwelling is a lot of work! I don't know what I would do without Margarita. Everything gets dirty quicker because of the air pollution. The first two days, I wore myself out answering the phone and the sidewalk buzzer. We had so many homens (meaning men, pronounced omens) coming around. There was the electrician, locksmith, telephone man, pool man, insurance man, the garbage man, and the landlord. The landlord did not earn any respect for the trick he pulled. After we had signed the rental agreement, he hired a gardener to pull out all the beautiful, mature plants that grew in the front and backyards. One of the trees he pulled out was the one that hung gracefully over the end of the swimming pool. It had white blossoms with yellow centers. The previous renter cried when she saw what had been done to her lovely yard. The landlord was just wanting our American Company to put in a freshly planted garden. Becky called these numerous men who were showing up so often, our good homens and bad omens. Even the guarda (guard) from the previous tenants kept showing up, wanting to be hired.

Becky and I went to the feira or outdoor market today and bought fruit and vegetables. It was interesting! They also had fish, octopus, eel, and various other unknowns. We asked Margarita about one wrinkly, green vegetable. She said to cook it with manteiga (butter) and salt and to eat it with a glass of water in one hand. We decided not to buy any of that. After we got home with our purchases, we were trying to decide what to cook for supper. I told Becky to figure out what to have while I tried to read the Portuguese instructions on how to wash the fruits and vegetables with Hydrosteril (the disinfectant that the company recommended)."

Sometimes I would walk to the weekly *feira* where I bought fresh fruit and vegetables from street vendors. The open-air market was only a few blocks away and it was full of interesting smells and sounds. The food came in all colors, shapes, and sizes, and some which I had never seen or heard of before. There were the yellow, star fruit, papaya, palmetto, and breadfruits which resembled the hedge balls I remembered from Illinois fence rows.

We had the opportunity to purchase meat and seafood, too, but seeing it hanging in the open air with an abundance of flies made me determined to only buy meat at the best indoor shopping places. Ray's company was very good about advising us on those things. Although, their advice about which dentist to choose was not the best.

The man spoke English, but that was the only thing he had going for him. I asked him how much it would cost to fix my tooth and he coyly said, "Oh, you just leave that between your husband and me." I should have gotten out of the dental chair and left but since he was recommended by the company, I stayed. I told Ray about it, then he called the man and found that my bill was exorbitant. Ray had to bargain with him. That was not the last time people tried to take advantage of us because we were Americans. They assumed all Americans were rich. The next dentist I went to was honest but spoke no English. He was a true gentleman. His first language was German, so we communicated in Portuguese which was a second language for both of us. His fees were very reasonable.

I sure missed Becky when she moved back to Illinois after her eighteenth birthday. She bolstered my courage by just being there—a great partner in the everyday adventures of living in a foreign country.

When one of the Caterpillar wives locked her keys in her

car, which was inevitable, or when one of our appliances broke down, we would call our husbands at the plant and they would send out Durival, one of the local employees who was also the rescuer of wives in distress.

After our first year, we were offered a paid flight back to the US for the annual month-long home leave. That was an exciting time for us since we hadn't seen any family members since Becky left in August. We always took empty suitcases back to Illinois to fill with shoes and socks, parts for our American appliances, medications, and a few food items that we couldn't get in Brazil. We had our annual medical checkups, did repairs on the Illinois house, and visited relatives. Ray usually had a work day or two to check in with the US plant. Home leave was much too hectic to call a vacation, so we could hardly wait for the few days that we saved to spend up north for a little rest and rejuvenation.

It was during that first home leave when we discovered our little plot of peace and quiet in Minnesota. We made an offer on the property and then we returned to Brazil.

Just two weeks later, I received a call from the States.
"Ola'" I said, picking up the phone.
"Hello. Is this Ray Thielbar?
"Yes."
"This is A-Woodland Realty in Ely, Minnesota"
"Who?" I asked.
"We showed you a plot of land near Ely a few weeks ago and you made an offer and put down some earnest money."
"Oh, yes."

"I'm calling to tell you that your offer has been accepted."

So, just like that, we were practically lake property owners. Our emotions went from, "Now what have we done?" to "Wow! We own that beautiful place in Minnesota." And just possibly, we might get to live there after our Brazil assignment was finished.

Caterpillar's São Paulo, Brazil, plant was in dire need of reorganization and modernizing. In January 1980, I was sent to Brazil with the assignment of combining the various and scattered operations of the metallurgical division, production, metallurgical lab, and planning and maintenance into one cohesive unit under one director. Me!

The fact that I had learned almost nothing of the Portuguese language prior to arriving in Brazil often led to confusing and sometimes hilarious communications. I soon decided I needed a bilingual secretary, someone who could help with translation from Portuguese to English. Once the hourly and salaried people working for me became convinced of my desire to learn the native language, they became more patient with my language education. Sometimes, the hourly operators, in their zeal to expand my vocabulary, would include words that cannot be included in this book. When I ran these "new words" past my secretary, there were times when her face would turn red as she explained the meanings. This whole language thing was called "immersion training" (dumping a gringo like me into a sea of people speaking a foreign language). It must have worked because the visiting Caterpillar management people were impressed when I was able to talk to operators on the floor during tours of the facility.

In the early '80s, the economy in Brazil took a nosedive, thus thwarting many of the plans for capital improvements. Rather than lay off workers, we offered our metallurgical capacity to outside manufacturers. During this time, I became aware of Tia (aunt) Edna's orphanage through our church. Her orphanage was operating at the poverty level and was in much need of repairs. My suggestion that our maintenance division could send some men to help with repairs was met with enthusiastic support from upper management.

The skills we provided included electricians, plumbers, and carpenters under the direction of a maintenance supervisor at no cost to the orphanage. The company agreed it was in their best interest to keep our employees busy rather than laying them off. It was gratifying to see the transformation in living conditions at the orphanage with the help of qualified, motivated men. Tia Edna and her orphaned kids were grateful for the assistance.

Periodically, visiting management from general offices would ask for presentations of progress toward our goals. Rather than making the presentations myself, I delegated that responsibility to the English-speaking members of my Brazilian management team. The standard practice said that the American in charge would make *the presentations but instead, I chose to delegate that to the nationals. This became a matter of pride for them that impressed our stateside visitors.*

One of the perks of living overseas was the opportunity to do some traveling. Since the company was paying to fly us back to the States for our month-long home leave every year, we would schedule a stop somewhere along the way. For a few extra dollars, we got to see a little more of our interesting world. One year, our stopover was at Manaus, on the Amazon River. We took a boat trip on the river and saw the Meeting of the Waters, where the "black" water of the Rio Negro merges

Backwaters of the Amazon River with Dugout Canoe

into the "white" water of the Amazon. The "white" water isn't white, but tan and it contains silt, especially where the rainforest has been cut, allowing erosion to occur. The black water is the clearest of the two. On the Manaus side of the river, there were shanties built over the edge of the water. Whole families lived in those shacks, complete with the predictable and picturesque laundry hanging out to dry.

One of the more interesting trips was the one we took in a dugout canoe, paddled by a native. We got to see a more intimate view of the river along the south shore where the roots of large trees were intertwined in peculiar shapes. We also took a short excursion by bus to see more of the area on the south side where the water had spread out during flood stage. On this bus trip, two other people and I wanted to say we swam in the Amazon, so we wore swimsuits under our clothes and were prepared to do this. In case you are wondering, we did not see a single piranha—the tiny but ferocious fish known for their ravenous feeding frenzies.

We also had plenty of places to explore on weekends, as well. One year, we served as chaperones for the high school Sunday school class at Met Chapel (later called Calvary International Church) and stayed for several days at a *fazenda* (farm). This was farther into the interior of Brazil, giving us an opportunity to see some of the rural life. This farm had a lot of horses that were used to care for the cattle. On the bus trip to the farm, we saw coffee plantations and some unusual trees, including eucalyptus.

One night, while sleeping on the floor at the *fazenda*, I felt something crawling on me. I brushed it away and brushed it away again. Whatever it was, there was more than one. Finally, I got up and turned on the bathroom light and was startled to see ants from the west wall to the east wall covering the floor, all marching in the same direction. The other chaperones who were sleeping on beds instead of the floor asked me about it and I told them we had ants. None of us had ever seen anything like it. They caused quite a disturbance! Everybody scrambled to get their shoes on and tried to figure out what to do. We got the girls outdoors and saw that the ants covered the ground and everything else in front of their forward march. We sent someone over to the other house to alert the men and boys. They, in turn, got the farmer up and he put poison out in the kitchen which meant we would have to clean it up before we could cook breakfast the next morning. The farmer said they were army ants.

If that ever happens again, I will know what to do. We didn't need to panic, put out poison, or take up our bedding. We just needed to get out of their way. If we would have left them alone, they would have marched through the area, consuming whatever it was they wanted. After an hour or so, it was over. There must be a life lesson there, somewhere. No matter how difficult the situation, this, too, shall pass. Sometimes literally.

Several times, we and some other Americans would hire drivers and take a couple of cars on day or overnight trips. Going to the beach was one of our favorite trips. At one of them, we encountered some monkeys and parrots living in the trees. We spent a couple of weekends visiting Rio de Janeiro, Copacabana Beach, *Pão de Açúcar* (sugar loaf mountain), and the massive statue of Christ with his arms outstretched over the city. There were destinations to buy china or other dinnerware, and whole villages that were famous for art in many forms, including handmade lace.

We took the trip of a lifetime with some of the other Caterpillar families when we went to see Foz do Iguaçu. This is one of the largest and most beautiful waterfalls in the world. The falls border Brazil, Argentina, and Paraná. We stayed in a lovely, old hotel on the Brazil side and listened to the windows rattle all night long as water poured over the horseshoe ledge of the falls, into what can only be described as a boiling cauldron (Caldera de Diablo also called Gargantua Del Diablo—Devil's Throat). One of the side trips took us to the top of the falls. By water! The six of us, plus some others, climbed into homemade long boats, powered by an outboard motor and were taken almost to the rim where the water had a deceptive feeling of slowness. I couldn't believe we were letting a stranger take us to this spot in this small watercraft. These were third world countries in the early 1980s and we could see we weren't in the good ole' USA anymore, with its emphasis on safety.

We traveled to Brasilia, Brazil's capital city in the center of the country, far away from commerce and highly populated cities. And on our way home to Illinois, we made some extra stops in Machu Picchu, Peru, the ancient Aztec city built on top of a mountain, Jamaica, and the islands of Trinidad and Tobago. In Jamaica, we walked up a much tamer waterfall and took a rafting trip down a picturesque, unspoiled river while a guide poled the raft. We also used our home leave for an extra stopover to see our son, Bruce, who was married with two children and living in California by this time.

I had to take a taxi, usually a Volkswagen Beetle, to buy groceries until we got a car for me. Taxi drivers, police, and most people drove Bugs, including the electric company. One day, I saw an extension ladder strapped to a VW Bug, so its driver could work on electrical lines. Driving a car in São Paulo was probably the most dangerous thing I ever attempted. Most of the people didn't obey the traffic rules, and where there were four-lane highways, they turned them into five lanes. Ray's company even advised us to avoid certain traffic lights. There were cameras set up at some of the main intersections and at the end of the year, if you had traffic offenses, you would receive a bill. One year, we were charged for running a stoplight and this was dated at the time of our month-long leave to the States. It turned out that someone from the plant had borrowed our car for the weekend.

I had always loved to walk but after a couple of uncomfortable jaunts, I decided I needed a car of my own. I decided to explore a shopping area a few miles from our house. I wandered along the sidewalk, peeking in stores, looking at clothing that was made for women much smaller-boned than me. I was curious about household linens and kitchen items, so I checked those out. I didn't need or want anything. Suddenly, as I picked up a small wooden object shaped like a fist, I looked up and saw a man staring at me. This was a temporary store that was merely an open tent. This man's eyes were extremely dark, and the look on his face was difficult to discern. Was it a look of contempt? Or even fear? I decided his eyes were asking me what *I* was doing there. That's when I realized that the items I was looking at were objects of some foreign religion. The man was right. I did not belong there.

Ray and Rose, Brazil years

The other hike that woke me up to the fact that I was not in Kansas (or Illinois) anymore was the last one I took alone in São Paulo. I learned about a Bible study at an apartment complex where a lot of American businessmen and women lived with their families. I don't know how far it was, just that it was a long walk. On one such trip to the study, I felt like I was in danger. First, I saw the homeless man who was locally known as the "crazy man." I had seen him before. Margarita told me he was "loco." He was a larger than average man with bushy, red hair. On that same walk, two trees dropped limbs as I walked under them. I don't remember that there was any wind blowing at the time. After Bible study, on my way home, a man pulled his car up in front of me. I guess he thought that only a prostitute would be walking this far alone. I just kept going and picked up my pace. I had not been afraid before this because I was young and strong.

I decided that I wouldn't go out exploring on foot anymore. It was time to have a car of my own. Ray chose a car for me that

Horse-drawn cart in São Paulo

some Americans were selling when they moved back to the States. This was a nice old Chevy with an automatic transmission. The only problem was that every time I washed this car, a rusty piece of car body would fall out onto the driveway.

Driving in São Paulo almost deserves a chapter of its own. Besides the ordinary cars and dilapidated trucks, it is common to see horse-drawn carts, motorcycles, bicycles, and pushcarts.

The people with carts were usually traveling up and down the residential streets, checking garbage bags or items put out for the taking. On the busy thoroughfares, people would crowd as many vehicles as possible into a single lane. Then they would speed up. Nobody seemed to notice the lines that were painted on the road.

One evening, we had planned to dine at one of the popular *churrascarias* with friends. Another word for these restaurants is *Rodizio. A rodizio* is an all-you-can-eat style steak house where waiters bring customers samples of many kinds of meat on skewers straight from the grill. Then they continue to bring meat until you tell them to stop. Usually, there are bowls of beans and rice or potatoes to pass around family style.

Our friends had planned to drive to our house and then we would go together to the restaurant for a grand adventure in dining. Since I didn't have to cook, I went ahead with my errands across town, although "town," in this case, was across the wide and busy avenue, *Vinte Tres de Maio*, a challenge in the best of times. I had a couple hours to complete these errands and would still have time to change before our friends arrived. I had just finished my tasks and had started home when the electricity went out citywide, leaving chaos at the stop lights. Most vehicles were stuck in traffic with no place to go and, of course, the streets were full. As far as I knew, cell phones weren't even invented yet.

I waited, along with everyone, hoping for a way out, or for the power to come back on. This was a one-way street and fortunately, I was in the so-called passing lane. I had been looking at my watch and realized I wasn't going to get home in time for our dinner date. Traffic was inching forward, along with the predictable group of impatient honkers, when I saw an opportunity. Pedestrians were all gathered at the bus stop, so nobody was on the sidewalk. We were coming up on a side street and I had an empty sidewalk in front of me that reached all the way to the intersection. So, I took it. I pulled my old Chevy up on the sidewalk and drove to the intersection and made a left turn. I was hoping that my excellent sense of direction would help me get home by taking some side streets. Interestingly, the side streets were nearly empty, so I headed in what I hoped was the right direction. Finally, I arrived home. Sometimes, it pays to break away from the crowd. I was over an hour late, but

Ray was entertaining the other couple in our dining room and they were probably wondering if they would ever see me again. We decided we didn't need to eat out that night and luckily, I had a couple of pizzas in the freezer, so we baked those. Then we tried to amuse our guests with stories about our first date when Ray had to drive down the sidewalk after the reverse gear went out in his car. Our planned adventure in dining turned into eating frozen pizza and the only adventures that night were driving in São Paulo traffic.

One Sunday evening after returning home from church, we found our front door open and a faint light glowing inside the kitchen. Some of Ray's tools from the garage were laid out near the door and a trapezoid window was open in the library. Muddy shoe tracks were beneath it on the wall. Obviously, the intruder must have been very small. The light in the kitchen turned out to be from the refrigerator door being left open. Some orange juice had been opened and a few items of food were taken. In the hall, Ray's camera bag had been emptied and the camera equipment was left where it was dumped. The bag was used to carry off every pair of blue jeans we owned, all of Ray's socks, all our sturdy shoes, and all my jewelry. We were thankful that nothing had been damaged or destroyed which we are told often happened. It was a bit unsettling to know that strangers had been in our house but considering what they took and didn't take, I was happy to share some of the bounty.

The next day, we asked around about getting a guard dog and we were directed to a family that raised German shepherds. We brought home a six-week-old, black-caped shepherd that fit in my two hands. He eventually grew so much that he was able to place his front paws on Ray's shoulders. Standing up. He was mostly black and was nearly invisible in the dark. Caterpillar also provided a block guard who patrolled the street every night. We grew fond of this guard and were happy to hear his greeting during the evenings. One morning, my maid, Margarita, arrived in tears. She had just learned that our street guard, *Joao*, had been killed the night before. We were the last of the Caterpillar families to live in a regular house. After we left, US families were encouraged to live in gated communities or high-rise buildings.

My days in Brazil were filled with Newcomers Club, book exchange, shopping, and teas with other Caterpillar wives. We also gathered on Sunday mornings at Calvary International Church, Dinners for Six and so on. One of the most fulfilling activities was meeting young Brazilians and sons and daughters of ex-patriots whose parents worked for international companies. We enjoyed having them in our home or offering them rides to church.

A lot of young men and women were anxious to try out their English at Calvary International. One special young man, Walter, learned English words in the car on the way to church, then on the way home, he would use the words he learned that morning in sentences. Truly amazing! Walter is a talented musician and a quick learner with a sharp wit. Our pastor and his wife adopted him, so he had the opportunity to study in the US. He is now an opera singer in São Paulo. We were privileged to get to know lots of young people. We couldn't help but wonder if some of these young people were the main reason God sent us to Brazil.

One of my contributions to our church was to write a newsletter for the many church members who were employees of multi-national companies or missionaries who moved all over the world. I also did some typing for ex-patriots who were writing books and prepared musical slideshows for missionaries to present on their trips to their supporting churches. We made some amazing and interesting friends in Brazil and remain in contact with quite a few of them thirty-some years later.

One Sunday morning when we arrived at church I was greeted by the pastor's wife. She asked if we might be interested in housing an American college student. I said ". . . maybe. We will talk about it." Becky was back in the States, so her room was available. Pastor's wife said the girl needed a place to go that night and we would be taking her home with us after church. Just like that. We said "OK. She can stay with us." Sometimes its best if we don't have too much time to think about a thing. She was a lovely girl and she stayed with us until a room became available at the college dorm.

The weather was very pleasant in São Paulo. I suppose that is because of the higher altitude. When we drove down to the beach, the air was noticeably much warmer. Normally, in the summer, we had a brief afternoon rain shower and then the sun would come back out. This was different than Illinois where clouds came in and then stayed for the whole day. Being too hot was not usually a problem. It was mostly the opposite. The houses were made of cement and none of them had built-in heat. We were advised to buy a portable propane heater which we used when the weather got colder than a sweater could remedy. On rare occasions, we had frost which could damage the flowers in our yard. *Neve*, the word for snow, was a part of the language, even though we never saw snow during the five and a half years we lived there.

When our assignment in Brazil was up, Ray was offered another contract for three to five years. It was a pretty good deal, since he got paid in cruzeiros as well as dollars, and dollars were valued highly at the time. But by then, the thought of three to five more years sounded more like a sentence than an offer. Our parents weren't getting any younger and we felt like our family needed us. Besides that, we missed our kids and we had a new adventure coming up in Minnesota. So, we packed up the bare minimum, sold our furniture and appliances, and asked Margarita what we should do with the things that didn't sell. She said she knew plenty of people who would love to have the rest of our belongings, so we delivered them to her house and left them for her to distribute.

We returned to Illinois in 1985 after spending five and a half years in South America. The Illinois house needed some repairs and upgrades, so we had some work to catch up on. It was difficult to concentrate on improving the Lacon house and yard because our hearts were already in Minnesota. Ray continued to work at Caterpillar and I finished up floor plans for the lake cabin.

A MEANDERING LANE

Rose and I had an idea for a meandering lane from our forest frontage road up to our building site. The lane would pass between two huge, stately pine trees that dwarfed all the surrounding forest. We would clear-cut the trees and brush that hid what we envisioned the lane to be, using only a 14-inch McCulloch chainsaw, an ax, several hand saws, some nippers, and some shovels.

We had noticed a worn footpath that passed one of the tall white pines and followed it over the ridge to the neighbor's place on the north. The neighbors had left a pencil and a notepad hanging by the front door, so we thought we would let them know we were building a road adjacent to their property.

One day, as we worked, we heard someone calling out to us. A man appeared on the path. He was showing some years but moving easily through the brush.

He introduced himself as Ken, our next-door neighbor. He had found our note and heard the sounds from our chainsaw. We learned that Ken had been a ranger working for the US Forest Service before his retirement. He now spent summers at his lakeside cabin.

In the days that followed, Rose and I enjoyed taking walks with this friendly summer resident. He seemed to have an intimate relationship with the local plants and animals and he freely shared his knowledge with us. We looked forward to his visits and his introduction to the ways of the forest, as well as the stories he told about the early residents at our lake. Use of that woodland path picked up considerably that first summer.

This historic path was here when we bought the acreage, used by the original owners of the old log cabins to the north and the south of us. This was also a game trail used by deer and bears. Our four-legged neighbors were likely keeping the path from completely closing, given that the original owners were gone. I once saw a moose come down that trail from the north onto the road that leads up our hill.

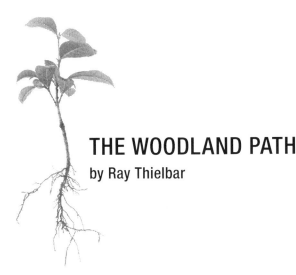

THE WOODLAND PATH

by Ray Thielbar

The Woodland Path

There's an old woodland path 'tween my
neighbor and me,
A path that's been etched over time.
Many footsteps have made the old path as it is,
Between my neighbor's log cabin and mine.

When needs have arisen at one end or the other,
A helping hand, or a tool or kind word,
Then the footsteps would tread this old worn
woodland path,
And a friendly "hello" would be heard.

The path gave no heed to whose footsteps it bore,
Neither seasons, or weather, or time.
It did its good deed in providing a way,
Between my neighbor's log cabin and mine.

BUILDING THE ROAD

To create this curvy road between two ancient pine trees, the engineer and the poet worked side by side with a vision, a chainsaw, and lots of bug repellant. The task might have seemed daunting if we had let ourselves stop to consider the work in front of us. The plan was for us to clear the lane of trees and brush, then call in a contractor with a bulldozer and backhoe to remove the stumps and bring in gravel to finish the road.

We had marked the roadway with bright pink surveyor's tape. The local army of mosquitoes must have gotten the word of our coming for when we arrived, we were met with a virtual swarm of the pesky critters. Rather than repel the bugs, our repellant seemed to be an attractant. Any exposed flesh became a target for these marauders. With mosquito netting around our heads, we began the work.

I met Ewald, the contractor recommended to us for the job, at the local bar in Winton. Picking him out in the bar was as effortless as I expected. One would imagine seeing a man cut from the same stuff as the obstinate ledge rock that dominates this wilderness landscape. His face was weathered as befitting a man who spends a lot of time outdoors. His hands were calloused and used to working with heavy equipment. It turned out the bar served as his "office," and if I needed to talk with him, this is where I could leave a message. I was impressed with his confidence and self-assurance.

His earthmoving equipment consisted of a Case crawler, a backhoe, and two 10-cubic-yard dump trucks. His equipment showed the scars of much use but was well maintained.

Our road builder arrived on-site and began dozing stumps and pushing them into a pile at the base of the rocky escarpment. Then he spread gravel from the beginning of our lane to the base of the challenging wall of rock. At one point, Ewald told me he needed to get on top of the hill. Climbing aboard his crawler, he approached the rocky hill and began to inch his way toward the top. A huge smile broke on his face as he rode his machine precariously, like an Olympian going where others with less courage would fear to go. As the cleated tracks fought for traction, I feared the machine would topple over backward, but Ewald was enjoying the ride. That hill, which became part of our lane, has been a challenge for those without four-wheel or all-wheel drive vehicles.

The first two improvements we made at the Minnesota building site after we had a road were an outdoor toilet and picnic table. Ray built both at our Illinois house and we trucked them up north in the pickup. We heard a few hoots and hollers as semi-trailers and cars passed this peculiar cargo. Ray also built a bench and placed it in a shady spot down by the water. Maybe once in a while we could sit there and just enjoy the moment. The future house site was just above the point that juts out into the lake, so there were views of water on three sides. We finally settled on a floor plan, and construction was scheduled to begin in 1987. We could hardly wait to start building the cabin. However, the canoe race that happened in Illinois in 1986 nearly put an end to those plans.

SECTION
4

Ray ready to paddle (in later years)

WINNING THE RACE,
WHILE LOSING HEART

The canoeists were hard-pressed to hold their canoes in some semblance of a line as they waited impatiently for the starting gun that would announce the beginning of another annual Henry to Lacon Canoe Race. The course started at the Henry Marina, ran an eight-mile route down the channel of the Illinois River, and ended at the Lacon Bridge. To make the course more challenging, there was a freshening crosswind out of the west on this particular day that would turn the surface of the river into a slight chop and make it difficult to hold our seventy-six-pound aluminum canoe on course.

During the previous week, Chris had been looking for a companion to paddle with him. Having won three previous races, he was aware of the strength and endurance levels required. I was a bit surprised, and a bit pleased, when he asked me to consider being his partner. My response was that I had doubts about my strength. Doesn't the Bible say something about pride going before a fall? In the eleven years since having heart bypass surgery, I had maintained a good diet, coupled with an active exercise regimen, including walking, jogging, bicycling, and canoeing. And that spring, my wife and I had clear-cut a 650-foot roadway through our wilderness acreage for a future building site. Nevertheless, I encouraged Chris to find someone younger than my fifty-one years, but he called me back and said it was me or no one.

We set our objectives and race plan. They were simple: win the race and break last year's record time of one hour and sixteen minutes that Chris had set. To do this, we would use short power strokes and feather the paddles during their forward arc through the air to reduce wind resistance. Chris would call out the count to change sides approximately every thirty strokes, saying, "One, two, three, change!"

The starting gun blasted, and we dug into the water with our paddles. The canoe lifted high in the water from the thrust and broke water at the bow as it surged forward. We could each sense the others' effort, as we put everything we had into gaining an early lead. Not only would this allow us to set our own pace and course, but it would also eliminate the psychological trauma of seeing someone else ahead of us.

"One, two, three, change!"

Every time we changed sides, it was a relief to my muscles. My right arm had begun to feel like lead. Immediately, the bow wave increased with our surge in velocity. We were both feeling good. Chris began to say how far ahead we were. The only response I could offer was to say, "Shut up and paddle."

Off to our right, the starter and his crew were keeping pace with us in his power boat. His crew included people who were trained in emergency medical procedures, including cardiopulmonary resuscitation. It was comforting to know they were there.

"One, two, three, change!"

I was sweating and beginning to tire, but in slightly less than thirty minutes into the race, we were crossing the halfway marker. We were on pace to set a record. Another five minutes passed. Then ten. I was straining to see the Lacon Bridge above the tree line. We had gained a comfortable lead ahead of our nearest competition. If we could just keep up this pace, we would go for our second objective of setting a record. I was tiring and beginning to wonder why I was punishing my body like this when I felt pain in the center of my chest. It felt like indigestion or a gas bubble that would go away if I could just rest awhile. My paddle strokes began to lose power and rhythm. Chris asked if I was OK. I called back that I was going to rest a bit but would help balance the canoe. "Just keep paddling," I said.

I could hear the racing starter crew in their motorboat draw near and ask if I was OK. I replied in the affirmative. I just needed to rest. I could sense Chris having problems keeping the canoe on course against the crosswind. I remained in a bent over position, low in the front of the canoe with my head between my legs. At times, the dull pain would nearly disappear, only to return. If I could just burp and relieve the pressure, I believed I would feel better.

It seemed like a long time before I could raise my head and finally see the Lacon Bridge looming above the trees. Looking back, I could see the competition gaining on us rapidly.

Meanwhile, I was standing under the Lacon Bridge with my bicycle and watching for the first canoe to appear upriver. It was late July and the weather was hot and muggy. I had expected them to do well and managed to get there early. I wasn't disappointed. The first canoe came around the bend and I raised my binoculars. Sure enough, it was Ray and Chris, and they were way out in front. Their big Grumman canoe had just rounded the island north of the bridge. As I continued to watch, and as other observers gathered, I noticed that another canoe was gaining on them. I began to fear they might lose their lead, so I hollered, "They're gaining on you! Paddle!"

Ray seemed to be resting but he picked up the paddle at my urging and then Chris shook his head and mouthed the word "No!" I immediately stopped cheering and waited. Something had to be wrong. Ray must be in trouble! And Chris, our strong, wonderful son, was bringing him in and winning the race at the same time.

Whether due to the rest or returning adrenalin, I began to feel better and determinedly set to paddling again. We crossed under the bridge ahead of the others by only a few minutes. I was too tired to even help Chris paddle to shore.

Their canoe slid into the boat landing just ahead of the others, and they were rewarded by a wave of the checkered flag and an Olympic style medal. At that point, people from the pick-up boat that held first responders also came in and rushed over to ask if Ray was OK.

He panted. "Yeah." Then he waved them off.

Oh. Maybe it is nothing. Sometimes he likes to be a little dramatic, I thought.

By then, Ray's mother had arrived and was waiting there with me. She said she had to run off to judge the kiddie parade, so I asked if she had her Nitro with her. She handed over the pill bottle and left without asking questions. I gave Ray a nitroglycerin tablet, then asked Chris if he could ride my bicycle home for me. It was just four blocks. He shrugged as if to say, "Sure, I just won an eight-mile canoe race single-handedly. No problem."

Someone must have given us a ride home in their car, I don't remember. By the time I got Ray home, he was doubled over.

"It's just indigestion," he kept saying. "If I can get rid of it, I'll be OK."

I wasted a few precious seconds, weighing our options. I had no car. The car was parked at the Henry, IL, Marina, eight miles up the river. I called our local ambulance and was told, "Sorry, the ambulance is out on a run." Most of the neighbors were downtown watching the parade. It was becoming obvious that I needed to get Ray to the hospital. "God, help us, please," I prayed.

By then, Rose had given me a second nitro tablet. Neither one did much to relieve the discomfort.

That's when Becky pulled into the driveway. "Thank you, Lord," I whispered. "Bot!" I called as I rushed to greet her. "I'm so glad you are here! I think we need to drive Dad to the hospital."

It was a thirty-five-mile drive and people have asked me, "How fast did she go?"

"Not nearly fast enough," I'd tell them. Of course, that was before Becky told us how fast she was actually driving.

When we got to the emergency room, I barked, "Chest pain and a history," like I'd heard on TV. They put him in a temporary waiting room. The staff seemed to have lots of people who needed attention, which concerned me. After what seemed like way too long, a doctor came and told us that it was a heart attack, so Ray was admitted to the hospital. After tests the next day, we learned he had lost some heart muscle.

I can't say this was a total surprise. Ray had already had quintuple bypass surgery before he was forty. He had been doing well—going to work and continuing with his busy life. He had been able to throw away his nitroglycerin bottle. We learned he'd need another quintuple bypass surgery, followed by months of therapy and recovery. Looking back on the events of that morning, I can see that the things that happened were more than just blind luck. What if Ray's mom had not been there with her nitro tablets? And what if Becky had not driven up in her car at that moment? This was clearly a God thing.

Ray's heart attack made us even more determined to make a new life with less stress for ourselves in the Northwoods. So back to the drawing board I went. I wrote to our cabin builder and postponed the beginning of construction on our log cabin for one year. Ray, in typical fashion, recovered quickly.

Then I went to income tax preparation school, so I would have a useful skill. Just in case. Taxes and bookkeeping were already my jobs in our marriage. I was never what you would call a math whiz, but I was good at following those vexing IRS instructions and had to keep up with tax laws to do our own taxes. After a year or two of preparing income tax returns with a calculator and a pencil, we bought our first computer. Before that, if someone stopped by, they would find me sitting at the table with streams of calculator paper rolled out across the table and down to the floor. My financial contribution did little more than keep me in computers. I was *so* ready for computers. They were the great equalizers. You can do so much and learn so much with a few strokes of the keyboard or mouse.

I set up budgets and "what-ifs." Ray recovered nicely and went on to work several more years but we both knew he would have to take an early retirement. We would live on his pension, finish the cabin as our time and money would allow, and live frugally in the woods.

The biggest draw to Minnesota was the clean air, clear lakes, and cool temperatures. Mornings were crisp and energizing, and we often awoke to the sounds of birds. Evenings began with spectacular sunsets from our west-facing view. The calls of the loon reminded us we were in the wild. This would be an environment where we could shed some of the stress of modern life, which likely contributed somewhat to Ray's heart problems. Although living well is important, "You can't outrun your genes," as Ray's cardiologist used to say. Ray was able to continue working for Cat for six years following his heart attack.

Following my heart attack and second quintuple bypass surgery in 1986, I asked the cardiologist what would happen if I needed additional surgery. Two quintuple bypass surgeries had used up two of the veins from my legs.

"Transplant would be the next option; however, you would be too old to be considered." His news was sobering, especially since I was only fifty years old.

With my blood circulation once again restored, and with it my energy, I returned to my normal active lifestyle. But returning to my former energy level would take longer. I was off work for a month but exercised and worked around the house to build strength and endurance. Rose was conscientious of the foods we ate. We realized the importance of a healthy diet. I was especially predisposed to high cholesterol because of my gene pool, but I never thought of myself with a black cloud hanging over me, threateningly. I don't think I ever asked the Lord, "Why me?" My faith remained strong. Besides, we had this wonderful adventure waiting for us to explore in Minnesota after delaying the construction of our log home for a year.

SECTION
5

The log cabin

THE LOG CABIN

We contracted with a local log builder to transform our designs into reality. The log shell, including walls and roof support structure, would be constructed at a building yard outside of Ely, Minnesota, where all the log joinery and pre-erection would take place. In the spring of 1988, Rose and I had our first look at the building under construction. It didn't have any openings for windows or doors, nor did it have a roof or floor. A small rectangular opening where the future north door would be located allowed entrance to the interior. With joinery

Cabin before window cutouts

work nearing completion, the logs would be pre-drilled for electrical wiring, numbered, and disassembled for transport to our building site.

The white pine logs were huge compared to the size of the building. The sun and rain were causing

Impressive joinery

the yellow/white of the freshly tooled logs to turn dark. After re-erection on our building site, the logs would require bleaching to remove any mold and to restore the look of fresh logs.

While the work on the building was underway, a masonry contractor installed forms on our site that followed the contours of the ledge rock in which cement would be poured. Cement blocks would complete the foundation. On top of the foundation, a construction crew installed plates, rim, and floor joists. The final preparation for the log building was the installation of three-quarter-inch plywood underlayment.

As we think back on these days of early construction, we regret not being on-site more frequently to enjoy the excitement of watching the delivery and erection of our cabin on its foundation. Fortunately, our neighbors, Jack and Rosemary, were on hand to record the transporting of the huge logs on a semi-trailer truck over a road not designed to accommodate a load of this length. Some of the logs were nearly forty feet long, and some were even longer. In some tight places, the truck driver's skill was tested as he made the sharp bends in the narrow road. This not only damaged some trees but also caused the loads of logs to nearly topple over. Several fifty-feet long logs had to be transported to the building site using a hydraulic crane. The final hill up to our site was particularly challenging because it contained sharp corners at both the top and bottom. Rosemary wrote to us to say it took her twenty minutes to drive our narrow, mile-long road behind the delivery trailer.

The modern design of our cabin encompassed the best of the old and the new. The aged white pine logs, twelve to twenty inches in diameter, were cut to fit together in the Scandinavian full-scribed method of the past to keep out the cold in winter and the heat in summer. The cabin rises eleven logs high and is close enough to the lake to be able to see the water but far enough away to blend with the surroundings. We didn't want to ruin anybody's view—neither residents nor those who might wish to paddle to a secluded spot.

Large windows on the south and skylights on the roof flooded the loft and the living room with sunlight. The kitchen, though equipped with a cast-off white enamel sink, also sported a new self-cleaning oven, and country blue tiles adorned the rustic countertop.

The outhouse that was perched at the end of a path has long since been supplanted by indoor plumbing, though it remains a relic of earlier times. The upstairs bathtub was an ancient cast-iron affair, complete with a weathered, newly refinished oak rim. We started with an antique pedestal sink on which we wasted a whopping $100. When reality dawned on us, we knew storage was more important than looking quaint, so Ray built a cabinet that would hold a sink basin plus all the necessaries. The old tub was a perfect match for our log home and is unrivaled in comfort and luxury. This was Ray's uncle's contribution to our project, and it had been stored in his barn.

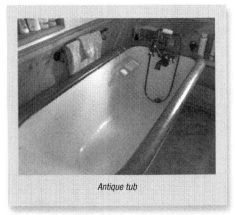
Antique tub

The downstairs bath also started with an antique clawfoot tub, which we purchased at an auction for $5.00. I'm glad the auctioneer didn't hear me whisper to Ray, "Let's go as high as $50." Years later, when my mom came to spend part of the summers with us, we took out the downstairs tub and installed a shower with a built-in-bench. I dread the day when I will have to give up my antique tub for the new shower. It does get a little more difficult every year to climb out of that deep tub, but what a reward it is to soak in it after a busy day of trying to keep the woods from overtaking the "yard."

The first floor has a bedroom, a bathroom, and a small but well-organized kitchen that is open to the dining/living room. The cathedral ceiling is almost high enough for a crow's nest or a tiny extra room. Of course, at this point, we wouldn't be able to climb up there, anyway. Sometimes, I imagine how I would design the place differently if I had to start over. The one thing I would do for sure is to make a catwalk in front of the tall south-facing windows to make them easier to clean. On second thought, I'd extend that catwalk over to the stairs and have an entire extra room.

A full-length porch faces the sunset on the west and an uncovered deck faces the south, which is nice for sunning in the early spring. Sometimes, we sit out there on the log bench in our coats and mukluks while snow is still on the ground. A deck on the driveway side wraps to connect with the porch. The second story houses the master bedroom, bathroom, and a loft for a TV/reading room with space in front of the bedroom for placing a long row of bookshelves. Electric cables and phone lines were buried underground so poles and wires are not visible. The feeling of wilderness remains.

We're on the grid, but out of sight. That was the goal. The problem? Running 700 feet of power cable through the wilderness from a power pole to our log home. The two options under consideration? Overhead or underground. Making the decision caused us quite a bit of head scratching.

The overhead option would require a thirty-foot-wide clearing through the woods. This would have to be maintained. Trees grow back quickly here. Our reaction? "No way." In building our lakeside log home, our desire was to make as little impact on the forest as possible. Clear-cutting would have left a large unwanted scar on the landscape.

The other option involved running power cables underground in an area notorious for hard ledge rock that came out of geological formations created eons ago by molten lava flows.

There are areas where ledge rock is at the surface; in other places, it is fissured and deep. We were somewhat aware of the problems of digging a trench through an area where ledge rock was abundant, but this is the option we chose. We had encountered ledge rock when laying out the location of our house. Since we had created a road through the wilderness to our place earlier, we chose to locate the trench in the middle of the road. The trench would need to be a minimum of two feet deep with the cable positioned in a bed of sand as a cushion.

But where could we purchase 700 feet of heavy cable and then transport it to the job site and lay it in the trench? With the help of an electrical engineer, we calculated the cable size that we would need to power our house with an acceptable voltage loss over the 700-foot run. An electrical supply house sold the cable to us on a large wooden drum. To transport the drum and cable 650 miles from Peoria to our log home in Ely, Minnesota, I built a trunnion in the back of our pickup. The trunnion would both support the drum and permit spooling the cable off the truck and into the trench at our log home. The five-foot diameter drum and cable that rested in the trunnion in our half-ton pickup that still had the canoe on top presented an impressive sight going down the highway. The camper, our temporary home, was trailing along behind.

Our contractor began trenching at the power pole with his backhoe. Progress up our hill was smooth as he continued working up our lane. At the top of our hill and heading toward our house, he encountered ledge rock. Using his backhoe, he located a detour around the ledge rock and completed the trench to the house. He placed sand in the trench. With one end of the cable attached to the backhoe bucket, he pulled the cable off the spool that was still located in the truck and laid it in the trench.

At the same time, we placed telephone cables in the trench. The operation was going smoothly until we ran out of cable about thirty feet short of the house. I had not allowed enough contingency to accommodate detours around ledge rock. Fortunately, I was able to locate enough cable of the same size to make a watertight splice and run the cable to the power panel located in the basement. We resolved the problem while sharing a few laughs and hugs to celebrate the occasion.

It was so easy to settle in and feel at home in our cozy log cabin. It has been a comfort to me to see wild animals continuing to live here as more and more humans stay all summer. At the same time, there is a certain excitement just knowing there are bears in the woods, a few elusive big cats, wolves, moose, and all manner of wild critters.

Since we decided to do the exterior painting, interior walls, and finishing work, progress was slow. We did the electrical wiring and plumbing in 1991. Up until then, all water, including the gallons and gallons it took to bleach every log in the building, was carried up the hill from the lake. Our cabin sits approximately forty feet higher than the lake, with a 250-foot path. Since we chose the house's location for the view, we had to build the dock in a spot with better lake access. Completed, it contains forty-five steps in two tiers of stairs in the steepest stretches. Ray's mother and I carried all that water and I used a garden sprayer strapped on my back to do the bleaching. Yes, this is the mother-in-law that I described "bulldozing her way through an incredibly busy life, singing at the top of her voice." Thank you, Mom.

Keith, a young friend who was an MK (missionary kid) that we met in Brazil, had come to the States to begin college. We brought him to Minnesota to help us do some work at the cabin. I think that was about the time we were staining the logs with a golden color. The brand name of the stain was Sikkens. A person cannot work with it without getting it on his or her clothing, hands, and hair. A little of that kind of work goes a long way in warm weather, so we decided to take a three-day canoe trip. Since we had some young muscle in Keith, we opted to take the 196-rod portage from Triangle Lake into the Kawishiwi River and paddled west, or down river.

We encountered a nice campsite that was close to the water with a place to climb up to a little overlook to watch the sunset. We did some exploring around the camp, and on our return trip up-river, the guys caught a nice northern pike. It was such a nice-sized fish that they named it Fred. We put him on a stringer but after dragging that poor fish upstream, Fred was dead. Rigor mortis had set in. We couldn't bring ourselves to eat Fred, but we did take him all the way home across that long muddy slog for burial in the vegetable garden. Ray and I never did learn to enjoy fishing. We always felt sorry for the fish. We do enjoy a fish dinner, however, especially when somebody else does the catching and cleaning.

Ray retired in the spring of 1992 at the age of fifty-six. He did some work for Caterpillar after he retired for two winters before we installed the furnace at the lake cabin. We spent our first full year in Minnesota in 1994. We had furnished the cabin gradually, bringing some new rummage sale finds with us on each trip from Illinois. Ray and I were walking around the neighborhood in Lacon one Saturday morning and noticed a nice white commode that someone had set curbside after doing a remodeling project. It was free for the taking. We finished our walk and came back with the car to pick it up. By the time we got back, someone had taken the ceramic lid from the water tank. The homeowner came out and said he was sorry. If he had known we wanted the stool, he would have saved the lid for us. Ray decided we should take the bottom part, anyway. Ray ended up carving a walnut water tank cover which made for a nice conversation piece.

Before that final trip up north, I packed my houseplants and the last of the items that were destined for the cabin. Unfortunately, our car broke down before we got there. I couldn't help but recall our proclamation that we made back in 1981: "If the car didn't break down too soon, our strength held up, and if we didn't lose our health insurance, we could afford to retire early and build our log cabin in the woods." *Uh, oh. That was two out of three.*

This was the first new car we had ever bought, so we were surprised when this happened on our way up north only seven years later. Ray was driving the old blue pickup. Every spare inch was loaded with household items. I was driving the Jeep which was also jam-packed. We were just reaching the outskirts of Superior, Wisconsin, when the Jeep started to leak oil and to smoke. We pulled over and asked where we might find a dealership which was handily just a few blocks away. We made it that far and had to leave the Jeep behind.

We had to choose which items to put in the passenger side of Ray's truck while still leaving room for me. We chose a few clothes, the groceries, and some of the plants which had to sit by my feet. The groceries sat on my lap the rest of the way to our cabin, which was about a three-hour drive. We left the rest of the plants in Superior. Thankfully, the guys at the dealership kept them watered while the Jeep was being repaired.

The log cabin is beautiful in a rustic, earthy way and fits nicely into the natural setting. Having said that, I can tell you where our cabin falls short.

If we had it to do over again, we would be there for the foundation's excavation. The space we marked out was all ledge rock, so we don't have a real basement. If we had chosen a spot just a few yards farther south, we might have gotten a basement with a third bedroom. As it is, our basement is merely a crawl space with barely enough headroom on the south side to house the furnace, the water heater, and electric panels.

Secondly, we would seriously consider making the cabin slightly larger. We don't have enough storage space in the cabin, but perhaps, having enough storage space is a fantasy. Maybe the more space we have, the more things we save. At this point, if we buy something new, we need to get rid of something old. It seems that our lives are bigger than this house. We didn't plan well as far as imagining how much our family would grow, either. We did, however, stay within a size we could afford. If someone asked me the advisability of building with logs, I would have to say, "If you can keep yourself young and fit enough to take care of a log cabin, then go for it." If you manage to live into old age, it may not be the house for you, unless, of course, you are financially able to hire people to do a lot of work.

PEACHES THE BEAR

Peaches was the best bear we ever knew. She was also the first bear we ever came to know as an individual. In the spring of 1992, we had seen quite a few bears in our many years as outdoor enthusiasts. None of the encounters had ever developed into more than a mere acquaintanceship. Not so with Peaches. Peaches was named by our neighbor, Jan, because of the animal's obvious enjoyment of that fruit. Peaches was not only a beautiful bear, she was an exceptionally nice bear. She was smallish in size, her hair was black, and her nose was a light brownish tan, except for the black tip at the end. She had a calm and docile disposition and didn't frighten easily. She pretty much ignored us once she grew accustomed to us and would walk around the yard even while we watched from the windows.

Peaches was not our bear, of course. She wasn't even Jan's bear or Rosemary's bear. Peaches was a wild black bear, and she lived in the woods somewhere near our homes on the lake. We never found where she slept or where she wintered, but she had a very distinct path through the woods. One day, we decided to follow the path to see where it led. We started out back at the bird feeder and followed the path through the red pines along the edge of the lake. The path to the north was fainter and less traveled than the south path, so we checked it first. It led from our compost pile to our neighbor's property on the north. We found a grease pit there where someone had buried cooking fat. From there, the trail went over the hill and intersected our lane. So, back we went up the hill to our house, starting at the bird feeder, which was a few yards away from the compost. This time we took the south trail.

The south trail was well traveled and easy to find—though sometimes we had to bend over to a near crawl to get under the fallen trees and brush. An animal could find lots of windfall in that section and we could imagine that a bear might just den up in there, though there were no signs of that. We followed the trail across the sunny blueberry patch, through the cool shade of the pines and down the hill toward Rosemary's cabin. We saw lots of tracks and smashed down grasses in one spot just north of the cabin. It was obvious that our bear had recently visited that spot. Then the path led around by the dock and through the cedars along the edge of the lake. Finally, this trail led to the kitchen side of Ray and Jan's cabin where there were many more tracks and bear signs.

Peaches had the gentlest disposition of any bear we have since come to know. She was a regular visitor that summer and would come by nearly every evening just before dark. We learned to anticipate her arrival, or sometimes Jan would telephone us to let us know the bear was headed our way. We were able to entertain our family and our guests with bear sightings from the cabin windows. Peaches taught us a lot.

Here are some of the things we learned from her. We don't have to be afraid of black bears. We never leave food or garbage outdoors unless we want a bear to visit. And while we would like for bears to visit, we don't do that anymore because it is hazardous to their health. We wash and recycle all cans, glass, plastic, and newspaper, and we don't store any of those items outdoors. We make a trip to the landfill every few months with refuse that cannot be recycled. We recycle everything else except for paper in which food has been wrapped. We burn that in the wood stove. All vegetable scraps go into a compost pile. We found that when a bear checks out the compost, he will rake it up nicely and that will aid in the process of decomposition by aerating and turning it.

We also learned that bears are always hungry and usually all they really want is food. If natural food such as berries, nuts, grubs, armyworms, and so forth are scarce, bears will come around more often. Most bears are more afraid of us than we are of them and will avoid us if possible. Bears are not nocturnal by nature and would rather forage for food in the daytime but will adapt to nighttime foraging if they need to. Bears have distinct personalities and they aren't all as even-tempered as Peaches.

Peaches never came back after that first year in 1992, though we continued to look for her. Always hoping. I don't like to think about the obvious, but Peaches was too good-natured for her own good. The last time any of us ever saw Peaches was two days before bear hunting season. Hunters did bag a bear on our road that year. I just hope that it wasn't Peaches.

BEARS AND OTHER CRITTERS

One of our first bear sightings on the property was a mother bear and her yearling cub. She seemed to enjoy the little meadow that resulted from our septic mound. I often watched from the window as she lay there with her cub.

One morning, Ray was busy building steps down to the lake. He had been digging and hammering log slabs into place and was totally engrossed in his work. Finally, he decided it was time for an iced tea break, so

North American Bear Center

he collected his tools and started up the hill. When he lifted his eyes toward the knoll, the mother bear and her cub were laying there in the path. The adult bear watched him with a mild curiosity, not unlike ours might be if we were observing one of our neighbors while he worked on a new construction project.

When the bear saw that Ray was starting to move up the hill, she gathered her cub and mom and cub quietly ambled off into the woods.

On another occasion, Ray and I were seated on our lounge chairs on the south deck, enjoying the sunshine and reading books. I looked up to see a bear coming down the path from the meadow, sensing her presence more than hearing it because she moved almost soundlessly.

"Here comes a bear," I whispered to Ray, then smiled.

Ray watched as the bear cautiously approached the deck, searching out all the spots where squirrels or chipmunks had stashed seeds. I sat motionless, waiting to see how close she would come. Ray, in the meantime, had gone after his camera and he snapped a couple of shots.

I continued to pretend to read. I sensed that I was completely safe, but usually bears didn't come that close. My chair was parked just a few inches away from the edge of the deck on the east side, and directly in front of the three-step staircase. The bear, probably not much bigger than me, placed her front paws on the first step. My pulse quickened but my curiosity was greater than my fear, so I just waited. I planned to speak quietly to the bear if she came closer. Then she placed a paw on the second step. Still, I waited. The stakes were higher than my husband was willing to risk, so he quietly stepped toward her and she backed down. I'll always wonder what she would have done if Ray hadn't interfered.

I used to rake the dirt in our yard and put out trimmings of fat under an upside-down flower pot to see what kind of tracks would be there the next morning. The idea of the heavy pot was to keep the ravens and the jays from carrying the food away. I was hoping there would be something left for the pine marten. The marten couldn't tip the pot over, but they could tunnel under it to retrieve the food.

One morning, the flower pot was turned over on its side, so we figured a bear had been there. A glance at the bird feeder confirmed the fact because every single sunflower seed, shells included, had been swept away. This happened about every two or three nights, and then one morning we saw bear scat.

"Yep," we said. "We have a bear."

Finally, we got to see the bear one morning. We watched as she turned over the clay pot and then noticed a wolf laying in the grass at the edge of the yard. The wolf appeared to be waiting for anything that might be left over. There wasn't much chance of that, so I wondered if this was the normal pecking order. I asked our friend, Lynn, the bear man, if that was the case. He confirmed it was.

The last week of May, a new bear showed up just before dark. She made herself at home and spent the whole evening with us, so we got a good look at her. She strolled into the yard, following her nose just like a grazing cow, fearless, yet with a mind-your-own-business attitude. She was a full-grown female bear, a fine-looking specimen with a typical black coat, comely face, and gentle black eyes. She had such a calm disposition, so we watched her with great interest. For her appetizer, she selected the suet from under the flower pot and followed that with sunflower seeds from the bird feeder. After she was sure she had cleaned up every edible morsel, she ambled off down the path in search of greener pastures. We had been watching from the dining room window with mixed feelings of amusement and financial misgivings since we knew that this could get expensive. After she left, Ray put out another supply of seeds for the flying squirrels that would be coming after dark.

Mrs. Bear was "no unenlightened bear," to quote Yogi, the cartoon bear. After we had settled into our evening routine, back she came to clean out the seed supply once again. This time, Ray opened the cabin door and chased her away, calling her a "rascally bear." She trotted off, still hungry, of course, but not wanting a socially embarrassing confrontation. I watched her from the upstairs windows as she circled around the cabin and cleverly approached the feeder from the other direction.

Since it was empty this time, she checked and rechecked it. Then she settled down under it and proceeded to groom herself. She reminded me of the German shepherd we acquired for protection after our house was robbed in Brazil. That dog was just a friendly puppy until he decided he needed to protect us. The bear that was visiting us that evening was actually more docile than our German Shepherd, but likely carried an extra hundred pounds. We were happy to watch from the window.

Every few minutes, Mrs. Bear would get up and look in the feeder again, full of hope. She did that for ten or twenty minutes and then quietly padded up onto the deck to check out what we had left out for the squirrels. I guess this was her dessert. After cleaning that up, she sprawled out on the deck as though she belonged there. If you had been walking by, you would have thought she was the family dog.

It was nearing our bedtime, so we stifled a yawn and left our visitor on the deck while we excused ourselves and retired to the upstairs. In a moment, her black form would vanish into the woods and become a part of the black night. We would see her again and we welcomed her. She was an especially nice bear, unlike a few others we had known.

Once, we had a big male bear pass through. He managed to take a bite out of the rubber on the back door of the pickup topper. That was the last time we left sunflower seeds in the truck overnight. Last year's bear got so nervous when she spotted us that she ran down the path, losing her water as she went. Then there was the bear that bluff charged us, chomped her jaws, and then ran and hid behind a small tree. It was difficult to take this bear seriously after witnessing her peering out from behind a skinny tree. But we treated her with respect and remained a courteous distance away.

We will always remember the summer of 1995 as the year of the drought, high temperatures, low water levels, and forest fires. Also, we will remember 1995 as a year of abundant bear stories and almost no blueberries. Our own private blueberry patch—which has yielded as much as seven blueberry pies, two batches of pancakes, and two batches of muffins annually—yielded just two berries that year. The bears were hungry and getting into more trouble than usual. One family returned home to find a bear enjoying the pleasures of their hot tub. Occasionally, a bear would rip into an old cabin to get to the termites or ants or whatever insects had taken up residence.

For those first few years we lived here, it became commonplace to see black bears nearly every day. One day, I was carrying the compost bucket out to the edge of the garden. I was walking from the west side of the house when I met a bear coming around the east side. We were both headed to the compost pile. We both stopped and looked at each other. The bear was smallish but healthy looking with a nice black coat. He started to turn around and go back the way he had come, so I softly said, "Hello bear." He stopped at the sound of my voice and turned his head to look at me. I spoke quietly, "It's OK, bear." He paused, satisfied that I wasn't a threat but decided to save his compost visit for another day. He calmly walked away.

One summer, our granddaughters were playing on the porch when a bear walked into the yard. The girls hid behind the big pine posts and peeked out at him. They said the bear played peekaboo with them. He would peer from behind a bush or a tree to see if the coast was clear before venturing out to raid the bird feeder. We heard lots of stories of bears showing up in town that summer. One lady said a mother bear and her two cubs came strutting past the Revenue Building and headed in the general direction of Zup's Grocery Store. She said it looked like any other mom taking her kids to town. My favorite story from that summer was of a resourceful bear who was caught pushing a dumpster full of garbage down the street in Duluth. Some enterprising photojournalist had captioned his work "Meals on Wheels."

We became involved in the North American Bear Center, doing our small part to take it from concept to reality. Ray was a member of the original board and I kept membership records. I wrote a monthly newsletter during the organization stage, and we included bear stories from our readers.

PEANUTS VS. SUNFLOWER SEEDS

The following life exper-
ience took place in the
early years of our residency
in bear country where we
are the intruders and the
bears are the residents.
It took us a while to learn
about bear behavior firsthand.
It is a lot like learning a

Ray and wild black bear on our property

second language in a foreign country. At the outset,
the learning curve is sharp and a struggle, but as time
goes on and one begins putting words together to form
sentences, the student finds new freedom. That's
how it was for us with bears. Our false perceptions
of bear behavior that depicted bears as fierce animals
were replaced with a new appreciation, respect, and
understanding of this wonderful animal.

On one occasion, a medium-sized male bear approached our place, no doubt drawn by the scent of peanuts in the shell. Rose had placed those on the ground just off our deck. I think the motive for placing the peanuts where she did was to distract the bear from the sunflower seeds in the bird feeder. Rose was upstairs when the bear appeared. I noticed the bear feeding on the peanuts and wanted to see if the bear had a preference between peanuts or sunflower seeds. I put some sunflower seeds in a bowl and quietly sat down on the top step that led off the deck while holding the bowl in my hands.

The staircase had nine steps. The bear caught the scent of the seeds and slowly approached the steps. I remained sitting quietly, holding the bowl as the bear mounted the steps. As he came closer, our eyes fixed on each other. The bear took the edge of the bowl in his jaws and gently pulled as though to say, "Let me have the seeds." Slowly, I emptied the bowl on the steps. The bear ate the seeds and returned to his peanut feast.

I was so caught up in the magic of the moment that I did not call Rose. My calling might have scared the bear away. Instead, I put some more seeds in the bowl and took my place on the steps while holding the bowl. Again, the bear left the peanuts, mounted the steps, and took the lip of the bowl in his jaws so I would give him the seeds. However, this time I chose not to empty the bowl but held on to it. The bear slowly moved forward, gently took my wrist in his jaws, thus encouraging me to give him the seeds. As I continued to hold the bowl, he took my forearm in his jaws ever so gently, communicating to me to give him the seeds. Which I did. When the seeds were gone, the bear returned to the peanuts. I was utterly euphoric about this experience, so I went into the house to tell Rose what had just transpired.

Some family members were expected to arrive soon. I told them about the encounter and asked that if the bear should come into the yard again, to have a camera ready. The opportunity presented itself, so I got the bowl with seeds, got down on my elbows and knees on the ground, and started approaching the bear. He got down on his elbows and watched as I got closer. As we looked in each other's eyes, I felt we were bonding in some way. I fed Mr. Bear out of my hand while someone snapped a photo.

That photo is the only record I have of this experience. Please don't try this yourself. This could have been the most foolish thing I have ever done and could have ended very differently. What if this had been a bear with no patience for a silly human's curiosity? We're still not sure if Mr. Bear preferred peanuts over sunflower seeds, but we're thinking he didn't much care.

As it turns out, we did no favor to the bears that frequented our place in those early years by feeding them. They easily become habituated to humans and to the food we provide, causing them to lose their fear of people. This can get them in trouble with people who do not appreciate bears quite as much as we do. This friendly bear did not appear at our place again. We heard a rumor that a nuisance bear had been shot on the other side of the lake that year. That made me feel sad.

Was it my actions that changed his normally cautious behavior?

PINE MARTEN

The first time we ever saw a pine marten, we didn't know what it was. His long luxurious black tail was hanging out of the bird feeder one night in such a way that made it look bigger than it really was. We were still camping out in our tent trailer

Pine marten

while the cabin was being built, so that probably added to the effect of making him look "bigger than life." I hurried to look him up in my critter book and I saw a fisher! Maybe. Then I saw a picture of a wolverine. It would've been so exciting if it had been a wolverine. But that wasn't the case. I also noticed weasels, mink, and ermine in the books but ruled those out because of their smaller size. Then I read in my 1959 mammal book about pine martens. It said martens are the owners of one of the world's choicest furs and that it wasn't likely that we would ever see one of these handsome animals in the woods. Obviously, I needed a newer animal book.

The second time I saw a marten, he was growling over an old dried banana peel from the compost one day in the early spring. Snow was still on the ground and he was obviously famished since he was making such a fuss over a blackened banana peel. I needed to get a better look at this creature, so I began to leave out scraps for him. I found that he loved meat scraps and suet but would eat sunflower seeds, bread, or dog food, too.

Once he began to lose his wariness and come around during daylight hours, I could see him much better. He was long, slim and quick, equally at home in a tree as on the ground. He was maybe two feet long and his tail appeared to be as long his body. A look through the field glasses revealed a yellowish white rim at the edge of his short, rounded ears. He also had a buff-colored patch on his throat. Several times we watched him take the suet from the limb of the spruce tree. He would hang on the plastic onion bag that contained the suet, gouge open a hole, stuff the entire contents into his mouth, and scamper off with it.

After we began to see more of these beautiful creatures, we saw that while all of them were similar, they varied quite a bit in color from light tan to reddish or near black. One year, one of the little fellows got so accustomed to us that he would allow us to replenish the bird feeder while he waited nearby. Another time, he ran right up on the porch when I was preparing to carry the compost bucket out. He had no fear of me at all and tried to get into the house. I hurriedly blocked him with my feet and stepped back inside. I am always mindful that contrary to their cuddly disguise, pine martens have scent glands, sharp claws, and sharp teeth.

Pine martens are fun to watch. They have long bodies and short legs. They will stand on their back legs, look this way and that, and then run and hop, doing their little pine marten dance. This particular one would stand on his two legs to get a better look at us, then fall back on all fours. I'm so happy they have made a comeback in our area.

FLYING SQUIRREL

One of our most interesting sightings was a flying squirrel. We had seen them before but had not seen them "fly" more than just a few feet, nothing more daring than the red squirrels do. But one night after the moon was up, we stepped out on the south deck to enjoy the sprinkle of rain that we were hoping would turn into a good ground soaker like we needed. It didn't rain, but a flying squirrel was clinging to the side of a big aspen tree. We watched him for a few minutes, admiring his oversized eyes. He ran up to the very top of the tree. Then suddenly, he jetted off like a tossed Frisbee and glided all the way across the clearing in our backyard.

The next morning, I went out with a tape measure to determine the distance on the ground from one tree to the other. I measured the angle to the top of the aspen and then using trigonometry, calculated that the squirrel "flew" eighty-five-and-a-half feet. Spectacular!

A LIVING JEWEL

In my hand I held a jewel—a precious, shimmering, emerald green. The underside was white with a patch as black as obsidian. The length of it was about three inches and its nature was so delicate that I needed to hold it gently, so I didn't cause it harm.

The black patch was changeable. It would radiate colors from buff orange to a brilliant ruby red. The glow seemed to come from within and would change from black to iridescent orange and red.

Ruby throated humming bird

My little gem had the ability to open its fragile gossamer wings, which hummed when he flew. And the way he flew was unique to those of his kind. He could fly extremely fast and he could fly both forward and backward. His courting flight was a large pendulum arc back and forth in a shining rainbow. He had a long beak and an even longer yellow tongue which would dart into the flowers to extract the nectar. He would then draw the tongue back into his mouth to consume the sweetness. He was especially fond of red. If we wore red clothing, he would buzz us like a mosquito to see if we were as sweet as we looked.

When he flew into my window and fell onto the deck of our house, I held him in my hand, trying to will my warmth and strength into his tiny body. And when the light went out of this precious living gem, tears streamed down my face.

VELOCIRAPTORS

A scream tore through the darkness and I strained to focus on something. Anything. Leaves in the jungle canopy above me moved ever so slightly. The darkness was tinged with a faint predawn pink. I struggled to move but my feet were tangled as if they were in a net. The heat and humidity made it difficult to breathe. I fought for consciousness. But I was floating, drifting, swaying with the leaves above me.

Velociraptor, crashed

A screech, like chalk on a blackboard grated overhead. The screech was echoed by a squawk. And another. There were clearly more than one of them. Prehistoric creatures? What? I knew the sound. Dinosaurs, maybe? A large bird. *Velociraptors!* The thought entered my preconscious state and I sat up with a start. Jurassic Park, the movie!

Where am I? I kicked my feet, finally breaking free of the blankets that had trapped me. I drew in a breath of fresh northern air and looked at the pine branches swaying in the skylight window in the ceiling over our bed. *Ah, yes. Raptors, indeed.* And, I was no longer living in South America. I looked Velociraptors up on a website just for fun and saw a photo of prehistoric bones and a drawing of what it would have looked like when alive.

Later, I discovered a gray tree stump at the edge of the woods with some twisted roots and limbs which looked very much like the artist's suggestions of what these dinosaur birds must have looked like. The stump was complete with a rock which I imagined might have brought the raptor down. I photographed it and titled it "Velociraptor—Crashed."

The first time we saw these hawk-like birds was in 1995, during the fall migration. A pair of small raptors of some kind had come by on their way south and had stayed with us for a week or so. We watched with interest since we didn't have many opportunities to view these birds. They were about twelve to fourteen inches in length. They looked brown from a distance, and we couldn't see any distinguishing marks, even with binoculars. They were clearly meat eaters and we wondered why they stayed at our place since the only food we had left out was sunflower seeds and a little suet.

Eventually, we figured out that our place is a regular smorgasbord for bird and rodent eaters since we have been feeding birds, squirrels, and chipmunks here for several years. One summer, after deciding that those raucous birds were suddenly louder than usual, I took a closer look.

Out in the top of a Norway pine near the trail to the dock, four of these big birds were perched. They were all about the same size but two were fluffier than the others and the fluffy ones were making all the noise. Every time one of the other birds came near, the fluffy ones would open their beaks and let out a pathetic series of squawks. Juvenile birds! Begging for food!

I walked farther into the woods and eventually found their large nest near the top of a white pine just north of our driveway, probably only twenty feet from where we park the truck. With the aid of an expert and his big spotting scope, we were finally able to put a real name to my "Velociraptors." We could see that our noisy birds had a vertical black mark down from their eyes identifying them as merlins.

We had watched them chase crows, ravens, and blue jays, all of which were bigger than themselves. I also saw them with smaller birds clutched in their talons. They are not the gentlest of our woodland creatures and maybe my first sleepy identification of them wasn't too far from the truth.

A BAT IN THE LOFT

A bat was in the upstairs loft, and black flies were bombarding the window screens like little heat-seeking missiles. The moon had a circle around it. My eyes did, too. I felt the wisp of air on my face again and heard the flutter of wings. That was not a mosquito! The digital clock glared 2:00 a.m. I could still get some sleep if the silly creature would just hang upside down from the ridge pole and eat bugs like he was supposed to. But no! He had to dive bomb my already bug-bitten head.

I got up and opened the door to the upper deck and turned on the outdoor light. Maybe the outside light would draw him out of our bedroom. Aha! There it was—a mini-Dracula all dressed in his long black cape. I grabbed the vacuum cleaner wand, the closest thing I could find with a long handle and proceeded to try to persuade the errant creature to exit through the door. Torn between not wanting to wake my mate and resenting the fact that I was up doing battle unassisted, I let out a muffled screech as the little mammal crashed into me.

"I thought you creatures had radar," I said through my teeth! "Can't you feel the draft coming in through that big doorway? Out with you!"

Finally, the bedlam was too much for my sleeping spouse. He roused just in time to see me accidentally hit and stun the poor creature with the vacuum wand. Honestly, I was only trying to get it to fly out the door. After all, any creature who eats bugs is a friend of mine. But now he was stunned, so circumstances required picking the poor creature up and scooping it out the door. With the aid of a couple of wadded tissues, Ray, my hero, assisted the little renegade and we watched it fly off into the great outdoors.

Sigh! Lights out. Peace and quiet. Sleep.

FOXY AUNT AGNES

I tossed out some small fat trimmings one day, knowing they would likely disappear before I could go back into the house. Gray jays and ravens were usually the first to arrive. This time

Red fox

I was surprised by what showed up. The porch is seven feet off the ground, so I could see her from above. It was a beautiful red fox. Her coat was red at the shoulders and sides, blending into gray on her lower back and tail. The backs of her ears were black with gray on the insides.

I snapped several photos while she searched the yard for scraps. In one of the snapshots, it looked like she posed for me. She sat among the rocks where I had made a dry waterfall and dry stream bed. She placed her black front feet together and spread her long tail to the side. Her beautiful black legs looked like she was wearing black stockings. It reminded me of a very old photograph of my Aunt Agnes who, as a young woman, sat with her sisters for the photographer. Agnes was wearing long black stockings.

Of course, I named this fox and will always think of her as Aunt Agnes. When she faced me, I could see that her neck and underparts were white. Her long bushy tail had a white tip. She didn't seem to be afraid of me, so this was especially exciting. Since she was being so cooperative, I looked for another meat scrap to toss out for her. She started to wander away while I was looking for the meat, so I whistled like I would for a dog and was rewarded with her prompt return. I couldn't wait for Ray to get home, so I could tell him about the fox.

When Ray rattled up the rutty driveway in his truck, she left. I described her to Ray, but I wanted him to see her. We went out on the porch and I whistled, as I had done earlier. We were surprised and delighted when she came trotting back, expecting another treat.

Aunt Agnes returned several times that week. I had just gotten a load of fresh garden dirt and had moved some of it to a shady spot where I planned to put hostas. She rolled in the fresh dirt and then laid there while I worked outside. When Ray and I were moving some of the new soil to the turn-around in the front yard, she sat down in the driveway and watched us. We pretended to ignore her and just continued with our projects. It was like having a dog. We wanted her to feel safe with us, but we didn't want her to begin to rely on us. We hoped we could just be good neighbors.

WHERE TO PARK THE CANOE

We needed a dock. How could we live the Northwoods life without a dock? And not just any dock. Ours would have to be out of the water to conform to a DNR ruling that prevented new permanent structures, including docks, in the lake.

At the time we chose to build the dock, our son, Chris, and nephew, Jerry, were planning to visit. Chris would be driving his Jeep. I secured a permit from the forest service to harvest two large white cedar trees at the edge of our property. One of the trees would serve as the front log, the other as part of the support structure. Using Chris's Jeep, we dragged the two trees out of the forest and up to our house. While Chris limbed and peeled the logs of bark and branches, Jerry and I cleared a path down the hill to the lake. The idea was to shove the log down the steep hill to the dock. Everything would be good provided the log didn't veer off course and lock up in a couple of trees in its direct path.

I placed a small log at the top of the hill to serve as a roller. The three of us hefted the end of the front log on the roller. Chris used his Jeep to push the log forward until gravity took over. The log picked up speed on its downward descent, narrowly missing the two trees. The inertia was so great that the log hit the water and floated well out onto the lake. Jerry swam out and retrieved the log and pulled it back to shore.

The site for the dock was in a shallow bay. Two rocks, one at either end of the bay, were conveniently located to serve as support for the front log. One rock even had a natural notch to accommodate the large end of the log. But we wondered how we were going to lift it. We didn't have any trees nearby to use as a hoist.

"Time to get physical," Chris said. He grabbed the big end of the log and, with Jerry's help, lifted it into place. The front log was long enough to span the mouth of the bay. We fitted the rest of the logs to provide the support for decking to complete the dock.

LANDSCAPING

The landscaping was kind of hit or miss since we mostly left the site in its natural state. The terrain is rocky and uneven, so I

Border garden

took advantage of all those rocks, digging them out with a spade in the so-called yard and the gardens. We built retaining walls in five different places and had a little precious dirt hauled in. I also took advantage of the native wildflowers which grow here and planted those in great bunches, especially the Shasta daisy, my favorite flower. We had vegetable gardens for a few years, having to change my gardening style from Illinois black dirt to almost no dirt in Minnesota. And then we had to adapt to the wild critters that seem to enjoy some of the same foods we like.

Eventually, we bought a nice-sized tractor with a bucket, which made an amazing wheelbarrow. We could dig up some of the larger rocks with it. Ray leveled a part of the yard on the south side, brought in some dirt, and built an actual yard where we sowed grass seed. Sometimes, we wonder why we did that since now we have grass that needs to be mowed. On the other side of that equation, we had volunteer grass and weeds that had to be weed-whacked, anyway. It really is easier to push a mower than to carry a heavy weed-whacker. It is interesting how much nicer a flower bed looks when it is set off by freshly mowed green grass.

One of the garden spots isn't really a flower garden. It is a dry stream bed. I put some of the rocks we dug out of the yard at the beginning of my dry stream bed to suggest a waterfall and a possible water supply. The rest of those extra rocks line the stream. The only time we have water there is when we have a heavy rain and it runs off the house in a nice gush out the downspout. We have about eleven flower beds. One is my woodland garden that borders the driveway on the north side, twisting among a stand of red pines. I moved wild ferns to use as a backdrop and purchased, or was given, perennials like foxglove, iris, and peonies. I added a few new perennials every year so that every garden plot had some splashes of color all summer.

We have another garden in the middle of the turn-around driveway. It has rocks, evergreens, and birch trees that we have planted flowers around. We also have a hosta garden on the lake side of the house and shade-loving annuals on the north side off the front deck. Wild ferns provide a backdrop for impatiens in various shades of pink and peach.

Our gardens on the south side have sun lovers like lupine, Joe Pye weed, white and yellow daisies, iris, evening primrose and lilies, and both Asian and daylilies. Asters and sedum are interspersed with the occasional red-leafed Spirea bush, and some tall blue bell-like flowers from the roadside. We have some hearty tansy growing here and there. It is not the best plant for flower beds because it grows four or five feet tall and it likes to multiply. It is not invasive, however, since it is possible to keep it under control, unlike some other plants. I think it is worth the trouble, so I have put it at the edges of gardens where it is OK to let it spread. It bears delightful golden flowers that bloom in late summer. They do have to be cut down at some point but can be left through fall and winter and keep their flowers after they have browned and dried.

One of the surprising things about living in the woods is how fast aspen and balsam trees grow. When aspens fall or are taken down, they will send up runners or roots underground in what seems like a frantic attempt to preserve the species. This requires snipping off little aspen trees all over the garden and yard. All summer. Every year. I am not a biologist, I'm just telling you what I see. The woods can literally grow in on you if you ignore those shoots too long. Aspen shoots often try to grow up under the deck. Another negative aspect to aspens is that since their roots are interwoven, they often fall in multiples.

One day, Ray, Chris, and I were trimming the lower dead limbs from the pines on the lakeside. Ray had given me a chainsaw lesson. But when I finished making a cut, I started to set the saw on the ground near my foot and realized that the business part of the saw was still moving. Yikes! That's when I decided I don't do chainsaws. So, there we were, Ray and Chris trimming branches with their chainsaws and me, using the branch lopper which does nothing automatically.

We loved this place in the woods and the trees *are* the woods, right? Meanwhile, Ray was sawing away with gusto. When Ray and Chris are together, competition happens. When I went to check on my husband, he was happily cutting a ten-foot swath clear to the ground. After waving to get his attention above the buzz of the saw, he noticed I was not happy. I asked him what he was doing. He said he wanted a better view of the lake. I told him I thought that the swath he had cut looked like a bowling alley.

WINTER IN THE WOODS

'Twas the night before winter
when all through the woods,
All the creatures were stirring,
still gathering food.

Ray had stacked firewood and
ordered propane,
My cupboards were full of
canned goods and grains.

"Winter's the best season,"
all the folks said,
So, we thought we'd try winter
and feeling no dread.

Decided to try it,
before we sold our old place.
"Can we live here year-round?"
That's the question we faced.

Our house is all cozy,
as warm as we want it,
And so far, the water
still runs out of the faucet.

What if the lights flicker
and down goes a wire?
We've still got our stove
to build a wood fire.

But building gifts for Christmas
out in the breeze,
Turns Dusty's (Ray's) fingers pale
and they threaten to freeze.

So, life would be easier if we had
our garage/shop
Before the big snows
decided to drop.

So, we ordered the boards,
the nails and the wood,
And we said to each other,
"So far, so good."

We then settled in for a long
night's sleep,
Still hoping the warm, fall-like
weather would keep.

We awoke the next morning,
and o' what a sight!
Our woodland had changed
from brown into white!

The ground was all covered with
new fallen snow,
So, we put on our boots
and with cheeks all aglow,

Set out to explore and look
at the tracks,
As we walked to the mailbox
with packs on our backs.

The road was all slippery
we soon found out,
So, we called up the supplier and
started to pout:

"Maybe your trucks can't drive
on our road!"
But they said, "It's too late,
They're bringing your load."

Well, they dumped all our wood at
the foot of our hill,
And I'm not too happy since
DELIVERED was stamped on the bill.

But we'll figure it out,
and we'll get by,
We can carry that stuff up the hill
if we try.

Then the winds came and
knocked some trees down,
So, we got out the chainsaw
to go into town.

Ray needed some material
so he got in the truck,
And headed for town
but he ended up stuck.

Crosswise in the road,
on a hill,
That truck wasn't moving.
'Twas just standing still.

We got our Explorer and a
long piece of rope.
Drove off to the rescue
with thoughts full of hope.

We got out of that one
with nary a scar,
And said to each other,
"Pretty good, so far!"

Next thing we know,
Monday morning arrives,
And here comes our builder in his
four-wheel drive.

Came right up our hill
with a load of our wood.
If anybody could make it,
Don, Kevin, and Dave could.

So, they set out to do it,
and it's a good bet,
that we'll have our garage
and we might make it yet!

There have only been about three times when we weren't able to get to town when we wanted to. During one such instance, we had a deep snow. We ran out of space to put the plowed snow and had to hire a bulldozer to dig us out. I'm not counting the time I tried to drive to town on glare ice and slid off the road. A snow-plow driver pulled me back onto the road, then I continued to town.

The second instance was when the culvert froze. Water started running over the road instead of under it. No railings were present at this crossing and it would have been a substantial drop from the road into the partially frozen water on the east side. We had gone to town for groceries that day and couldn't drive over the build-up of ice, so we walked home and brought the sled to pull the perishables across.

The third time we couldn't get to town happened years later, after a storm, but that story deserves a chapter of its own.

A few times, someone got stuck in the snow, but eventually, we were able to get out with the aid of our other vehicle or by calling our trusty neighbor, Bill. One time, the old plow-truck got stuck on the hill with the blind corner. We still had my car available, but how do you rescue

Log cabin in snow, as viewed from the garage

a truck from behind with a smaller vehicle? The road was icy, and we couldn't get the car around the truck to try and pull it. Not easily discouraged, we got a long rope, hooked it on the front of the truck, took the end of the rope around a tree that was in front of the truck, and brought the rope to the front of my car which was behind the truck, and hooked it on. I slowly backed up my car, hoping the smallish tree would hold. It held, and it allowed us to pull the truck out of the ditch just far enough that Ray could drive it up the hill. We have since used that method several times for stranded delivery trucks, too.

GOLDEN MOMENTS FROM 1993

Amy and Julie at Orr general store

August has been filled with golden moments. You know the ones: you're out in the canoe, the sun is warm, the water is cool, the only sound is the swish of your paddle. You wish every day could be like this, but you know it won't. It's the kind of moment you store up inside to help you weather the uncertain days. There were some other golden moments that first year after Ray retired. Our granddaughter, Amy, was snuggled up against me, telling me her dreams in the middle of the night; hearing Julie's infectious laugh, and watching these girls embrace life with such gusto. The bear visit that I told you about when he came within a few feet of me as I sat reading on the deck happened in August. And the yellow daisies were in full and riotous bloom!

September has also been an extraordinary month. We did more fun things in September than we did the rest of the summer. I don't know if it was the weather, our frame of mind, or simply the fact that Ray's saw broke down. Since Ray could no longer use his saw, there was a more relaxed atmosphere about the place. This was more of what I expected retirement on a northern lake to be like. My son-in-law accused me of sabotaging the saw. When we wrote our young friend Keith, and mentioned the saw being out of commission, he replied that he thought I wouldn't sabotage the saw but wondered if I might have made it a matter of prayer.

We took a three-day canoe trip, several hikes, explored Jewel Lake, took a course in plant identification at the college, had two or three picnics, had folks over for dinner, and we ate out. We went to see the wild bears at the Vince Shute Wildlife Sanctuary up in Orr, where bears had been coming in the evening for decades. Dozens of bears hung out just as they had done back in the days of the logging camp. Since then, someone decided it would be wise to separate the bears and the humans and built a viewing platform. I'm so glad we got to experience walking with bears before they built the viewing deck.

As the month progressed, we celebrated a neighbor's birthday, rented some movies, read some good books, and sat in the sun and enjoyed this wonderful season in the woods.

Fall is a delightful time to live in the Northwoods. The air takes on a brisk feeling and the sky is a deeper blue. Maple leaves start to change from green to red. The spirea bushes turn red, along with other shrubs in the woods, then the birch and aspen turn to yellow and gold. The whole countryside takes on a golden glow. Even when it is raining, the yellow leaves make us think the sun is shining. It's a kind of optical illusion, like using the color Yellow Light in an oil painting.

Some of these golden moments came about when a theory we had about drop-in company was tested by Becky and her family. We wrote about this subject in the September-October 1993 issue of our family newsletter, *The Homefront.* We did a survey, asking whether a person preferred invited company where you plan, clean, and cook until you are so exhausted you can't enjoy your guests. Or do you prefer unplanned company which allows you to relax and let the visitors help scrounge for meals, and you get to stay in your favorite paint-splattered shirt? The consensus was that an hour's warning is best. You have just enough time to fix your hair and change your shirt. If you are quick, you might have time to sweep the front porch and take a package of hamburger out of the freezer, as well. But you don't have time to wear yourself out cleaning the house and baking up a storm.

In the example above, Becky and family, who lived about twelve hours away, called a few miles south of Duluth and said they would be here in three hours. We had invited neighbors for lunch that day, so the house was reasonably clean. We had leftovers in the refrigerator. So, how did we use that three-hour notice? We relaxed and rested.

It was one of the more enjoyable visits we have had. We got to feed squirrels and chipmunks with the girls, went exploring, took the Bog Walk near Orr, saw some black bears, found a few late blueberries, gathered wildflowers, and played computer games. After the girls are all grown up, we will still have these priceless memories.

THE WOODBOX

I enjoy the nickname Rose hung on me a couple of years ago. "Dusty" describes what I do or make, sort of. And to hear her tell it, there is always an abundance of it around. Sawdust, that is. She doesn't like it too well when my sawdust gets tracked into the house. And when we are expecting company, I just know I might as well clean up my mess because she'll tell me to if I don't.

Ray carving a sign

One of the problems I have is geographical. My "shop" is the porch off the cabin we built, so any woodworking I do out there is bound to show up in the house. If I just had a shop away from the house, I could dust myself off in the space between before entering the cabin. But as it is, any dusting off I do just falls onto the porch and gets tracked in. Or if there is a breeze, it gets blown in. And there we go again!

I suppose if I build a garage/shop as we are planning to do, I'll have to clean it up, too, before company comes. Sometimes it's tough living up to a nickname.

We built the garage in 1994. We had spent whole summers at the cabin after Ray retired in '92 but hadn't installed a furnace until '93, so we were ready to try winter. The garage plan that we chose provided for a sleeping room above the garage. This would come in handy for the kids. Our three kids had married, and their families had multiplied to nine by then with more to come. In the room over the garage, we installed electricity and a propane heater, but it doesn't have water, so you can't really call it a bedroom. Ray uses the room for his drafting table and stained-glass work.

While Ray was busy in the shop making sawdust, I was busy moving wild daisies around. Wild daisies have quite a few advantages: they thrive in Minnesota; they stay fresh looking through most of the summer; and they are free. The roots are shallow, so you can easily dig them up and transplant them. And they reseed themselves. It's no wonder the kids started calling us Dusty and Daisy.

Our son, Bruce, carved a "Thielbar" sign for us as soon as our cabin went up. I liked it and thought I could do this. This seems to be the beginning of sign carving for me. I think one of my first signs was the one hanging off the corner of my shop, "The

Woodbox." I made it from a leftover remnant of a log that was used in the construction of our house. The Woodbox became the name of my sign business. The first sign for an Ely business was the very popular "Bear Paw Books" on Chapman Street. People loved the book store and the woodsy sign, so I never had to advertise. As a retiree, word of mouth provided all the work I wanted.

HOT AND DRY

I hardly heard a sound—hadn't heard one for days. The heat hung in the air like a sinister presence. The sun was shining but the air had a hazy quality to it. Even the usually chattering squirrels lay like limp rags on the tree limbs. It was too quiet in the woods. The balsam needles were turning brown and asters lay in a withering heap. All of nature panted for rain. Temperatures had risen to 101 degrees and stayed in the 90s for weeks with no relief in sight. Even the nights were hot. It was rather unusual for northern Minnesota.

The hummingbirds and the dragonflies sought relief from the drought by playing in the sprinkles from the hose when I watered the garden. Twice I watched a woodpecker take a dust bath in the driveway. I dragged a dust cloth over the furniture, trying not to raise a sweat as I awaited Ray's arrival. It was still 98 degrees. Each time I passed a window, I would check the billowing white clouds of smoke that loomed across the river to the south of us. *Forest fire!* Maybe three or four miles away.

It had been burning for weeks, but the clouds seemed bigger today and the wind was picking up. I could smell it now. Wood smoke.

I hadn't seen a large animal in days. Thinking they may have the right idea, I began to form an evacuation plan. I would watch the wind direction, and if necessary, would put my computer tower in a box and grab some clothes, shoes, and the checkbook and be ready to leave in a hurry. Thankfully, Ray arrived safely and the next week brought three or four good heavy rains. The Forest Service reported that the fires were out. Temperatures had gone down by thirty or forty degrees, and the squirrels began to chase each other around again. Another sure sign that things were beginning to get back to normal was that we saw another bear. He was a little thing, probably out on his own for the first time. He came around every evening after we scraped off our supper dishes onto the compost.

The first night he showed up, a red squirrel chased him off, but he began to grow accustomed to us and no longer ran off at the first squeak of a floorboard. He was so short he couldn't quite reach the sunflower seeds in the bird feeder, so he grabbed ahold of the feeder with his forefeet and boosted himself up with his hind feet onto the trunk of the spruce tree. Then he would hang by his paws and lick up the seeds with his long tongue. He was so adorable! It was a comfort to see him come around every evening. The woods felt safer after the bears came back.

We've seen several forest fires during the years since we lived in the woods. One year, we noticed a float plane had touched down on our lake and then took off right away. A few minutes later, we heard the plane return and this time we watched as the pilot dipped a large water bucket into the lake water and carried it off to the south of us. When he returned so quickly, we realized that there must be a fire nearby. Much too close!

The sound of a pontoon-equipped beaver (airplane, that is) dropping onto our lake with a water pod slung between the floats caught our attention. The pilot was picking up water and dropping it just out of sight over the tree line. In a matter of minutes, the plane would return to pick up another load of water, indicating that the fire was nearby. So, Rose and I hopped in the motorboat, picked up neighbors, Ray and Jan, and motored across the lake to see where the fire was. We took the quick roller portage into Triangle Lake and discovered that the fire was burning on an island. It was started by an unattended campfire. This was possibly less than a mile from our cabin.

Even a small fire in the hot dry conditions of such a strange summer could be dangerous. Fortunately, the fire was spotted and two beavers, along with a five-man ground crew, were called to put it down. What would ole' Dusty do if there weren't any trees left for making sawdust!?!

Another fire was one we learned about in the middle of the night. We had just sat down to supper when we heard a loud boom. We thought it was probably a lightning strike, so we didn't think much about it. The neighbors called later that night to let us know there was a fire on the west side of our lake and that they had called the fire department. Prevailing winds come from the southwest. The fire department is sixteen miles southwest in Ely and we only have one road out.

The next day, we paddled over to see how much damage had been done and found the cabin had been destroyed by fire. To our untrained eyes, it seemed that the propane tanks must have ignited. Someone had stored an aluminum canoe inside the cabin and it had melted into a misshapen mass. We were glad the neighbors had called the fire department.

REVERSE CABIN FEVER

I had been retired less than two years when I got a phone call from Caterpillar.

"Hi, Ray. Are you tired of retirement yet? Would you be interested in working part-time interviewing job applicants?"

Two days of training preceded several months of very interesting work (more fun than work), interviewing applicants at Caterpillar's Central Hiring Agency. I decided to continue working at this enjoyable job during the few months that we spent in Illinois during winter.

We had installed a wood stove that took up a good-sized portion of our living room at the cabin. It was not the best arrangement but was adequate for all but the coldest part of the winter. In 1994 we installed a propane furnace, so we would be able to spend the entire winter in Minnesota.

It was September and the birch and aspen leaves were still green. But a change was in the air. A kind of dangerous excitement—a warning that summer was almost gone, and we had much to do before winter set in.

I was grumpy and irritable and experiencing a vague sadness. Whenever someone invited us to something in town (or anywhere besides our cabin), I felt desperate to guard the few weeks we had left. After two or three days of this undiagnosed malady, I recognized it for what it was. Only summer residents (or former summer residents) would recognize it.

Though our accomplishments were many, we still had things on our mental do-list that we hadn't finished: canoe trips, nature photography, and exploring. Then, of course, there was the unending yardwork and unfinished cabin projects that could only be done in summer.

The birds and the animals felt it too, this feeling of change. Warblers were coming through again and the chickadees and nuthatches were back at the feeder already. Hummingbirds were refueling before their long flight south. Red squirrels, which had been hoarding sunflower seeds ever since we arrived in May, appeared to have doubled their efforts in the past several weeks, jumping from limb to limb, breaking off pine cones, scolding anybody and everybody with their noisy chatter and chasing each other so skillfully through the tall pines. The black bear was back at the feeder every day now that the berries were gone.

The bush honeysuckle and the sarsaparilla leaves had turned yellow while maple leaves dappled the woods with red. Fall was in the air. As the evenings cooled, I warmed up on the inside with this strange affliction: Reverse Cabin Fever.

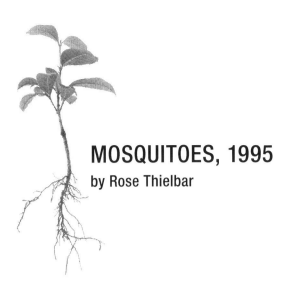

MOSQUITOES, 1995
by Rose Thielbar

'Twas early October down at the dock.
The morning was warm, so I paused from my walk.
N'er was a summer so scorchingly dry!
Wildfire smoke lingered for months in the sky.

There was something good about this dry year.
There were fewer mosquitoes buzzing my ear.
Believe it or not, some days there weren't any!
When it comes to mosquitoes, not any is plenty!

We had a good freeze to knock those pests out.
But here was a new swarm flying about.
The thing that's peculiar about this late batch,
They're so feeble and frail their eggs may not hatch.

Can you believe it? Mosquitoes this small?
Too weak to lay eggs and just hatched this fall.
Dare I to dream it? Hey, what do you think?
By nineteen ninety-six, mosquitoes extinct?

I see you're worried about our feathered friends.
It's no laughing matter if a whole species ends.
What will birds eat if mosquitoes all die?
I don't see a problem. Let them eat black flies!

WOODS MUSIC

The October woods were dusted with a light snow, and sunlight twinkled off yellow aspen leaves. Melting snow dripped rhythmically from the roof of our cabin as the sun rounded the tops of the balsam thicket. Chickadees, nuthatches, and jays were busily tuning up for their winter chorus, and squirrels were scolding with their guttural vibrations as they sang their parts in turn.

Chubs, the chipmunk, was perched on a mossy rock sounding his treble voiced "Chip . . . chip . . . chip" as the shadow of a large bird passed overhead. The tune from *The Sound of Music* danced through my mind as I listened, watched, and savored the moment.

Just as I looked out the dining room window toward the lake, a yellow-gray coyote tiptoed silently up the path, leaving tracks in the melting snow. His bright eyes were intent on the lower tree limbs and he stood upright, bobbing back and forth like the star of some ancient ballet. This whole incredible scene played out in a matter of seconds until he noticed that he was being watched, causing him to trot into the woods once again. It was a brief and magical moment, but the music and the scene are etched in my memory—the memory of the woods that beautiful morning that were "alive with the sound of music."

ROOTS IN A JAR

We took those woodland memories with us back to Illinois where we would spend a couple of months working during the winter. One particular year, I took my ivy plant back to Illinois so it wouldn't freeze after we shut the cabin down for the rest of the winter. The leaves fell off during the trip, which was not surprising since the temperature was -30 degrees at the time. I made cuttings from the vines and put them in an antique milk bottle and placed it on the kitchen counter where it could get some sun. This house where our kids grew up belongs to our daughter's family now. We would be their guests for 3 months. In a matter of weeks, I had some lovely starts with roots showing through the glass. This plant deserved special attention since it came from a plant my mother had since her early married days 61 years before. Mom made sure my sister and I had starts from her plant, so we could keep it going long after she was gone.

We celebrated my parent's anniversary that year by attending the church where they were married in 1935 and where we attended as a family for many years. This was the old Bricktown Church out in the middle of farm country. As we drove along the country roads, Dad pointed out places that held special memories for him and Mom. He even pointed to a pasture where my grandfather met my grandmother. There is very little evidence left that there had ever been a home there. Except for all of us! We had ample opportunities that year to think about our origins since we had three funerals to attend. Two were for elderly beloved aunts and one for a classmate of mine—one of the first to go from the class of 1956.

Recently, we cut down the huge maple tree in the backyard in Illinois. The tree was about forty-two inches across, and the branches towered above the two-story house. We counted forty-seven rings in the stump and spent time reminiscing about when the tree was just a volunteer sapling, growing in the fence row thirty-nine years before. This was an uncommon tree because it held a swing and several versions of tree houses through the years. The problem was, grass would never grow under it. I suppose the roots were too near the surface and so during the drought years of the '80s, this tree was not able to survive.

Roots are interesting things to contemplate. Sometimes a plant can be uprooted and do even better in a new location. Some plants wither and die if they are moved. Maybe some plants need more sunlight or more shade or are not hearty in certain conditions and temperatures. Our roots, the Thielbar's and the Braun's, can be traced back to farm country in Germany, in four short generations. There must be more to roots than the place of birth, however. Most of us have longings for home, and sometimes home is a feeling as much as a place. You know how you can pull a camper to a faraway place and once you have it set up, you have that favorite pillow, the beat-up camp pot, family members and routines which help to recreate that wonderful feeling of home?

We lived in that house for more than twenty-three years before the Brazil assignment but now it is no longer home. Now, home is wilderness with trees and water, clean air, and animals that roam free. Home is where I can hear the wind rustling the leaves of the quaking aspen. Now, the sounds of traffic are foreign. My connections are to the woods, to the very earth itself. The past three months have held precious moments that we've spent with our families, and I loved spending time with our kids and grandkids, but this house is not home anymore. I am an ivy cutting with my stems in a jar, just waiting to sink these roots into the soil of the Northwoods once again!

ICE-OUT

On April 25, 1996, six inches of new snow dumped onto our already snow-covered landscape, bringing the total snowfall to 118 inches for the season. Somehow, we managed to arrive back in Ely at the height of that snowstorm. The windshield wipers were going full-speed, visibility was diminishing quickly, and the Fernberg Trail was rapidly disappearing into a world of white.

Trees were heavy with the new snow and leaned into our roadway the last mile of our journey. We had brought along our old toboggan to pull our perishables along with my houseplants up to the cabin in case we were not able to drive the whole distance. But the untimely snowstorm didn't dampen the thrill of coming home. We were anticipating being there for the arrival of spring and especially "ice-out."

Much to our delight, the truck cleared our hill which was the last obstacle in our path. This would put the truck in

Ice-out

position to pull my car the last ten feet, so, thankfully, we were able to unload our belongings at the door. Just two weeks later, temps had warmed considerably, and a lot of the snow was gone. Our lane still had snow on it and a big drift was piled up at the front door. Ice continued to cover most of the big lakes, including Lake Superior.

By Monday morning, our lake had begun to open on the east side. Our neighbor, Art, was out paddling his canoe around the opening at the edge of the lake.

By Tuesday, May 14th, the backwaters were open. The temperatures rose to the mid-50s and the sun was shining. An open spot formed in the middle of the lake and a pair of loons swam at the edge of the ice, occasionally popping up in an opening, twenty or thirty feet from the shore. The open water had a black look to it and the ice had turned to white slush. A wind had sprung up and pine boughs were swaying. By midday, clouds concealed the sun. The wind had begun to push the ice into the north and east ends of the lake and the south side was opening. Chipped ice was piling up on the islands and waves of crushed ice were forced onto the shore. Out in the middle of the lake, the wind blew scoops of broken crystals on top of or beneath the ice flows. Gulls were riding on the flows and appeared to be enjoying their own private "fishing opener."

The whole surface of the lake was on the move as ice was piled upon ice. To hear the wonderful crystal chimes of crushing ice above the sound of the wind, you had to be at the water's edge. We knew that the ice would be gone by evening, so we watched in awe and admiration as winter gave her final performance before bowing out just in time for the entrance of spring.

SUDDENLY IT'S SPRING

The next morning, we awoke to sunshine and bird songs sweeter than any I had ever heard. I pulled on a sweatshirt and went out on the south deck. Ray had already been up and had put a fresh supply of sunflower seeds in the feeder. Prior to this, we had mostly been seeing juncos, chickadees, and sometimes evening grosbeaks. But on this day, the spruce and aspen trees were full of purple finches. One little brown and red bird started a song, a sort of tentative solo, and then soon, the

Fox

flock of twenty or thirty little birds joined in the chorus. The song built to a crescendo, a joyous triumph of survival. How appropriate for the day after the ice out.

I sat on the log bench and gave the amazing concert my full attention. Then suddenly, as if on cue, all the birds stopped singing at once. It was like the end of a concert. *Where is the applause?* I wanted to come to my feet and shout, "Bravo!" I couldn't help myself. I clapped my hands. The poor little birds were startled and flew away. I guess they really weren't singing just for me, after all.

SUMMER GUESTS

We love living here in God's country, but we do miss being closer to our kids. Becky is the closest at 640 miles. She, Seth, their kids, and maybe some friends usually visit us in late July or early August.

We needed to prepare for summer guests. We only have two bedrooms in the house, so someone must sleep in the guest cabin or the sleeping room over the garage. If necessary, we pop up the camper because it has two beds. Assignments are first come, first choice. I usually start planning menus before we start cleaning and making beds in all the places I just mentioned. I have a templet for typing up menus and I print them to use as a grocery list. One of the first things some of the kids do after they arrive is to check out the menu plans. That suits me. If they don't like my choices, we encourage them to make suggestions. Deciding *what* to cook is the hardest part of meal planning. The grocery store is sixteen miles away, so we don't want to have to make too many unnecessary trips to town.

Ray and I have worked out a nice arrangement when we have summer guests. He cooks breakfast and I prepare the other meals, usually with the help of family members. Everybody pitches in to help with washing dishes. When the kids call to let us know their travel dates, I ask them if they have any meal requests. They have three favorites: Grandpa's apple pancakes, Grandpa's spaghetti, and Grandpa's scrambled eggs. It is easy to see who the favorite cook is in this family.

CHEF RAY'S
SPECIAL FOOD FAVORITES

I'm not sure how preparing breakfasts became my responsibility when we had guests or family, but quite frankly, I enjoy the job. I am a morning person, so getting up before the guests is no big deal. It is normally quiet, the kitchen is mine, and the sun is likely just peeping over the treetops in the east, ready to throw her beams against the far shores like a contemporary artist throwing paints of various colors against a clean white canvas. Once in a while, I can even hear a loon's call echoing between the shores, making it difficult to determine where the call is coming from. Yes, mornings are a special time of day!

During our sixty-plus years of marriage, my wife, Rose, has taught me a lot of things about hosting a meal, including which way the sharp edge of the knife points when setting the table. Also, color is important in the presentation of food. She taught me some basic food preparation tips. She probably started with scrambled eggs. I mean, how can you mess up making scrambled eggs? Right? Being a person with an engineer's mind I decided to add a few of my own concoctions to the basic scrambled egg, thus developing what is now known as:

Grandpa's Scrambled Eggs

2-3 strips bacon
1/4 c milk per person
White onion, diced (as much as you like)
Salt and pepper
Green pepper, diced (as much as you like)
2 large eggs per person

Start by laying two or three strips of bacon in a large nonstick skillet, setting the heat to medium. Use a glass lid to contain the splatters from the bacon. It'll let you visually check progress while you dice some white onions and green bell peppers. Whisk eggs, milk, garlic salt, and coarse black pepper together in a separate bowl. When the bacon is fried to your desired crispness, drain all but about a tablespoon of bacon grease. With the skillet set back on the burner, still set at medium, add the diced onion and peppers as well as several pats of butter. I have found that butter produces a fluffier scrambled egg than margarine, and the bacon grease adds its own distinct taste. When the onions look transparent, slowly add the whisked egg, milk, garlic salt and pepper mixture. As the eggs cook, fluff them periodically until they are ready to serve. Then top the whole thing with grated parmesan cheese. (We always serve these scrambled eggs with local Zup's Italian Sausage and the heartiest bread we can find to toast.)

Grandpa's Apple Pancakes
(makes 14 small pancakes)

2 C baking mix   2 eggs
2 or 3 raw apples, sliced   2 tsp baking soda
Dash of lemon juice   2 T canola oil
Sugar and cinnamon mix   1 tsp vanilla
1 C milk   4 T sugar

If you like to make a mess, this is an ideal recipe to accomplish that purpose. For more than two people, I make the batter per the directions on the baking mix box, using the additional ingredients listed under "ultimate pancakes" (baking soda, vegetable oil, vanilla

Apple pancakes

extract, lemon juice, and sugar). Cut several apples; Gala are my favorites (they don't seem to brown as easily) into one-fourth inch thick slices (leaving the peeling on for more fiber.) Preheat an electric skillet to 350 degrees and add enough canola oil to coat the bottom. Add batter to the hot skillet to make pancakes about six inches in diameter. When the pancakes are slightly firm on the bottom, add apple slices to the tops of the pancakes. I usually add three slices per pancake. Lightly coat the tops of the pancakes and apple slices with a mixture of sugar and cinnamon. When the bottoms of the pancakes are lightly brown, turn them over using a wide pancake turner. When thoroughly cooked, remove pancakes to a serving dish. Place them on the table with sides of syrup, butter, and yogurt.

Grandpa's spaghetti

1 lg. pkg. extra lean hamburger,
   (about 1 to 1½ lb.)
1 med. white onion
1 can Italian blend diced tomatoes
2 cans tomato sauce
Rosemary leaves, salt, Italian Seasoning, oregano and basil to taste.
  Serve with garlic toast (butter & garlic salt)

As with most of my culinary delights, I don't typically use exact measurements of ingredients with spaghetti. Taste test is my guide. (Rose taught me that, too.) This recipe will serve six people with enough sauce for leftovers. I like to use a large electric skillet for making spaghetti sauce. Some prefer heavy cast-iron cookware. Preheat the skillet to 300 degrees and coat the bottom with canola oil. Dice a medium sized white onion into the skillet and saute it until it is well cooked. Add one pound of ground beef and dice it until there are no large chunks. Work the onions into the beef and cook thoroughly. Add one can of Italian blend diced tomatoes, and two cans of tomato sauce. Stir until it is well blended. Add salt, Italian seasoning, oregano, sweet basil, and rosemary leaves to taste. Simmer until all the ingredients are well blended, stirring occasionally.

In the meantime, preheat the oven to 350 degrees, slice some Italian or French bread, coat both sides with butter, sprinkle it lightly with California style garlic salt, and place it in a shallow baking pan. Bake until it's brown on one side, turn it over and bake until the other side is brown. As an alternative, you can use the oven broiler. This requires close observation to avoid charring the bread.

Add a teaspoon of olive oil to a large saucepan of boiling water. Add angel hair pasta and boil it until it is soft. Pour contents into a large colander and rinse, using a hot water spray. Fluff to avoid the noodles sticking together.

To serve, place angel hair pasta on a large plate and add a generous serving of sauce to the pasta. Serve it with Italian bread.

GRAY AND BROWN

The last of our summer guests had gone. Looking out the window, it looked like our world was mostly gray and brown with bare earth and bare trees—a kind of in-between time. Even the lake was gray beneath streaks of gray clouds. Frost had taken the last of the daisies, and the formerly bright yellow tansies looked forlorn in their coats of brown. The crumpled aspen and birch leaves laid on the ground beneath stark gray trunks.

The light dusting of snow which fell during the night had already melted under the morning sun, and the air was crisp enough that you could see your breath. The squirrels, snuggled away in their hiding places, were keeping warm in their new thick winter coats. We didn't see much bird or animal activity that morning and our world seemed eerily silent. But the green needles of the pine and balsam reminded us that life was still around us. It merely lays hidden for a season.

Out on the rocky rise, east of the cabin, a small weasel (or ermine), scurried from rock to rock trying not to be seen. His brownish fur was mottled with patches of white, and soon he would change into his beautiful winter wear, all white except for the black tip of his tail.

Any day the snow would begin to accumulate, and some morning, we would awaken to find our lake dressed all in diamonds and crystal. The brown and gray earth will be adorned in brilliant white. A new season will have arrived.

ICE-UP

By the time mid-November rolls around, the first thing we do when we get up is to see if the lake has frozen over yet. It would be easy for us to miss what locals call "ice-up" since it usually happens at night and since we don't have the intimate relationship with the lake that our neighbor, Will, had. Since he lived on an island, Will, had to cross the lake every day to pick up his mail or to make the occasional trip to town. Whether he crossed by canoe or snowshoe depended on whether our lake was ice or water. On days when the ice was too thin to walk on or too thick to paddle through, Will borrowed our "Grumman icebreaker" (aluminum canoe) or he took a few days to do some traveling.

We do get some warning that ice is coming. Mud puddles get a thin layer of ice on top. The shallower lakes or ponds freeze next, followed by the deeper lakes.

One year in early November, Will came over to borrow the Grumman. "The ice is getting thick," he said. "It feels like paddling in syrup."

We couldn't help but admire our friend's courage and stamina. We were somewhat envious of his closer connection to nature, but on the other hand, we could imagine pushing that aluminum canoe on thin ice and not being nimble enough to jump into the canoe before we slipped through the fragile layer between air and water. Ice-up is one phenomenon we are happy to view from our window.

JANUARY WARMUP

Sunlight melted the frost off the glass on the porch door, erasing the etched look, and opening our view to blue skies. Outside, toward the north, snow drifts were piled chest high along the path between the cabin and the garage. It was January, after all, even though temperatures soared into the twenties.

To our south, the lake was a field of white, looking more like a windswept tundra than a lake. Swirls of snow laid in random patterns, seemingly untouched from this distance. In the shadows of the afternoon sun, the trees across the lake appeared a burnt umber. Closer to the house and still in the sunshine, the red and white pines were a lively green with tufts of snow still clinging to the branches. The roof to the deer feeder wore a derby of two to three feet of condensed powder, rounded and shaped by wind and sun. Deer tracks lay across the yard in no pattern at all.

The quaking aspens, now leafless, no longer quivered in the wind but were enlivened with a grand display of our winter birds.

Evening grosbeaks and goldfinches once more added gold to the bare limbs where yellow leaves once clung. In keeping with the holiday spirit, touches of red and blue adorned the trees from pine grosbeaks and purple finches to gray and blue jays. The smaller chickadees, nuthatches, and pine siskins reminded me of the twinkling lights which decorated our Christmas tree, as they moved back and forth between the feeder and the tree limbs, drawing our eyes to first one branch and then another in a flurry of perpetual motion.

As enjoyable as all of this was to take in, some aspects of a Minnesota winter can be sobering. One night, we had to make the sixteen-mile drive into town for choir practice at 8:00 p.m. That is pretty late to be traveling when the temperature is -25 degrees and the north wind is blowing up a windchill factor of -55 degrees.

A small amount of fresh snow swirled across Fernberg Road, reminding us that we couldn't take anything for granted out here. We knew we could get to town. Getting home was going to be questionable, though. Conditions can change in a matter of minutes. We were glad we had worn our long underwear and warm mukluks and had tossed in an old blanket, just in case.

Halfway to town, we looked for the deer kill from a few days earlier. That was the second deer we had seen taken by wolves so far that winter. Thanks to the common raven, there wasn't a clue left at the scene.

Now that we had our own snow blade for the truck, the biggest worry was the possibility of running out of propane. The delivery truck drivers don't like our scenic road. It's a peculiar thing. That winding narrow tree-canopied trail we call our road is probably the thing that sold us on buying this property. I remember the first time we drove down that road. What a thrill it was—that feeling of entering the wilderness! After all these years of driving that dirt road we still experience the thrill of coming home to the woods. And in winter, with that steep hill of ours, coming home is still a thrill. Thrilled not just because we are home, but because we made it all the way up the hill!

During the winter in which I'm writing this, we're not experiencing record-breaking weather but -25 degrees with strong arctic winds out of the north, gusting to 30 mph, is still enough to get my attention. I can always tell when it is cold if I keep feeding the wood stove in the garage and can barely get the thermometer into the comfort zone.

As I have grown older, my fingers and toes have become more sensitive to the cold and they are quick to tell me when they have been inadequately protected. Severe conditions like these cause me to appreciate the invisible bonds between us and others who we have come to love and call friends who care about us and, for example, insist we call to confirm our safe arrival at our remote home after a meeting. And we appreciate those who ask about our health, especially as we brave the winters at our cabin. It's a cozy feeling when people ask if we have enough firewood or if our snowplow is up to the job. It's good to know we're never really alone out here in the woodlands.

Our forest friends, the deer, the red squirrels, the pine marten, and the various birds, confirm we are not alone, especially during the winter months when natural food is scarce. They keep us busy filling their feeders. We are rewarded as we view the animal activity through the window. Life here is not dull. Now, if I could just get the temperature in the garage above 40 degrees, I could go out and make sawdust.

Ray's invention of a squirrel-proof bird feeder deserves some comment. Everyone who has ever had a bird feeder knows that squirrels love sunflower seeds just as much as the birds do. Probably more. However, there is one difference. Squirrels take many more seeds at a time than birds do, and where they store those seeds makes a person with a frugal personality a bit disgruntled. In the summer, a large percent of those seeds sprout as spindly sunflowers everywhere and seldom mature enough to produce seed. If the squirrels had planted the seeds together in a sunflower garden, somewhere away from the vegetable plantings, this could be a good thing. We could have our vegetables and a patch of sunflowers, too. It's the wastefulness that gets to a person.

Squirrels are exceptionally clever animals. They can climb a post or walk out on the end of a fragile tree branch. If that isn't possible, they climb to a spot from which they can launch onto the platform of the feeder. The bird feeder that Ray engineered has smooth aluminum sheeting on four sides, so no toe-holds are available. It may not look as attractive as the all wooden feeders, but it does the job. Squirrels cannot get past the sections of aluminum, no matter how many times they try. And try, they do.

One might think my engineer husband would be congratulating himself on the success of his invention. But on closer inspection, one can see two or three little piles of sunflower seeds placed under the feeder for those poor, pathetic, hungry, little rodents. I just smile to myself and contemplate my guy's softheartedness competing with his desire to solve a problem. He built a successful barrier to keep the squirrels out of the feeder, but he gives them food, anyway. This way, everybody wins!

BACK TO THE REAL WORLD

One Friday morning in January 1996, we stepped out of our Christmas card world at the lake and drove back into the cold cruel "real" world. We drove the 640 miles back to Illinois and arrived that evening, weary but grateful to have made a safe trip on winter roads.

I suppose a reality check from time to time is good for us but suddenly we didn't have any more quiet evenings by the fire, and no more leisure hours of critter watching. Instead of sitting around sipping hot cider and watching deer and martens out our window, we had jobs and mountains of laundry and dirty dishes. Ray drove the thirty-plus plus miles to work while I wrestled with people's tax returns.

Our conversations went from the lofty thoughts of life in the woods and projects in Dusty's workshop to such mundane subjects as who needs the bathroom first in the morning, broken appliances, car payments, deadlines, and earache medicine. And since we were guests of our daughter and her family, we tried to fit in by helping any way that we could. Our three girls had saved eight months' worth of fix-it projects for us and I think there must have been almost that much laundry. In fact, I wouldn't be surprised if the neighbors were sneaking in some laundry during the night. I don't understand where it all came from. I just know that if you turned your back on it for more than twenty-four hours, it multiplied.

Evenings were filled with family dinners (it's amazing how much food such little people can eat), school activity reports, and homework. And instead of spending the evening playing Upwords or reading *The Tales of the North,* we played checkers or read bedtime stories.

Being back in Illinois is a pretty good life. Living in the "real" world is not as peaceful as living in the woods but we always received big warm hugs from little arms, engaged in fascinating conversations, got compliments on my cooking, and heard the little ones declare their love for Ray and me. And we got to examine new artwork on the fridge every day. We would be headed back to our Christmas card world soon enough.

One winter, ole Dusty had to go through an adjustment period. In January, we had to temporarily close our Northwoods log home. We had two feet of snow on the roof, the temperature was minus 23 degrees and later it dropped to −60.

We arrived at the Lacon house that winter where I went from quiet solitude to the loving attention of two vigorous little girls. And I went from a day without a schedule to a more structured environment at Caterpillar where it was fast-paced, and the day was full of decision-making. I actually enjoyed the change. Also, my dust-making capability at the Lacon house was limited since most of my tools were up north.

Someone supposedly said, "Change is good." I reckon there is some truth to that. Change does sharpen one's values of what is important and what is not. And I think change offers us some choices. Either I can accept it as an opportunity and smile or I can fear it for its unknowns and frown. I guess I will keep smiling.

OUT IN THE WOODSHOP

Out in the woodworking shop, there was evidence of a new undertaking; a large sign for the International Wolf Center. This project began more than a year earlier, when out of the blue, I received a call from the renowned wolf biologist and vice chairman of the center, asking if I would build a sign. I am still at a loss to explain how he got my name. Silly me, without asking what he had in mind, I agreed to make the sign. I later learned he wanted an eight-feet-long sign with three carved running wolves across the top. I had never done anything that big before. I learned my lesson. Always explore, as best you can, the path in front of you before starting your journey.

Three running wolves carved by Ray

It is not that I hadn't had previous opportunities to learn this lesson. Several instances come to mind. As a young boy of thirteen years, the outboard boat racing bug caught my attention. I didn't have funds to buy a boat, so I built my own. My first attempt was not the most successful. Oh, the craft was seaworthy; it just wasn't a racing boat. That's when I started to build a flat-bottomed hydroplane boat. They are a bouncy vessel, but they skim over the water on the Illinois River.

Ray at North American Bear Center, Ely, MN with one of his carved signs

I made another large sign, this time for the North American Bear Center west of town. Those two signs became the bookends to our "end of the road" town. Over time, I made more signs, both business and residential. In the meantime, I built us a king-sized log bed.

THE DOMINO EFFECT

Have you ever noticed how the addition of one new piece of furniture sets off a whole chain of events? Ray was busy in the shop building a king-sized log bed for the master bedroom. The logs were prepped and ready to cut to the proper length, but first, we needed to buy the mattress set and frame so this would all fit together. We knew that the delivery men would carry those huge pieces upstairs for us but before they could do that, we had a staggering amount of work to do, given that we were both in our sixties. By the time we finished, we had moved every piece of furniture in the whole house, except for the living room sofa and the dining room table and chairs.

First, we moved the best double bed and nightstand from upstairs to the downstairs guest room. The guest bed went to the garage sleeping loft, and the former orange crate/nightstand went to the porch. The extra bed went to some friends who run a resort, and the mattress with the springs poking up about hip level went to the dump. The removal of the extra bed left a lovely empty space in the master bedroom, which meant we could finally bring the good office furniture up from Illinois.

Meanwhile, I moved a table and chairs up from the overcrowded living room. Some of the good office furniture replaced the particle board work center in the guest room. The "temporary" work center went to the master bedroom along with the good bookcase. Then came the complicated job of moving the computer and peripherals upstairs, which created a need for a new phone jack.

After that, we moved the table in the bedroom to the TV/reading loft, which meant we had to move everything in the loft. That included a sofa bed, two chairs, a coffee table, and an entertainment center. That meant we needed to install more plug-ins. When we moved the chairs, it created a need for a lampstand, so I took the painted orange crate from the downstairs bathroom which created the loss of storage space in the bath. I put the painted orange crate back in the bath and moved the orange crate/nightstand from the porch upstairs to the loft.

Then, of course, the new larger bed needed to have larger sheets and bedspread, which meant trying to match existing curtains or making new ones. Fortunately, I found a new quilt that had pieces of the material identical to that in my curtains, so we didn't need to change the curtains. The quilt, however, while a perfect match, was a little skimpy, so I had to buy more curtain material to make a bed skirt.

Once we finished, the bedroom looked so nice that it made the curtains in the bathroom look tacky, so while I had the sewing machine out, I made new curtains for the bathroom. After the bathroom curtains matched the bedroom, the towels did not match the curtains, so I purchased a couple of new towels in the new color. Then I thought it was time to replace the orange crate with a new wicker towel cabinet. The bedrooms and the upper bath looked pretty good then. The dominos stopped falling, at least momentarily. Though, now that I see how nice the wicker looks in the upper bathroom, I'm thinking how nice wicker would look in the lower bathroom.

SUMMER WITH JENNY AND CHRIS

There is nothing like having young folks around to keep you on your toes. We swam, canoed, or motor boated nearly every day of the three weeks Jenny and Chris, two of our grandkids, spent with us. We made a trip to Lake Superior, explored the waterfalls at Tettegouche State Park, and hiked out to Shovel Point to watch the waves break against the shore and feel the cool spray of water from the big lake. We got to see a black bear up close in our yard. We canoed to see Indian pictographs and pitcher plants at Hegman Lake and motorboated up to Canada. We cut and stacked a couple of dead trees, worked on my

California meets Minnesota

"beach," hosted a wiener roast for our church youth group, watched some movies, and played games in the evenings.

My "beach" might need some explaining since it's nothing but sharp rocks where the land meets the water. I removed enough rocks to make a small space at the edge of the lake, so a person could enter the water barefooted. It is about the size of two farmgirl-sized feet. It just seemed logical to me that if we removed enough rocks, maybe a little sand could wash up there to fill the void. Prevailing winds come from the southwest, so that would be in our favor. Ray and the kids led me down there one afternoon to show me a surprise they had prepared for me. They had removed a few more rocks and added a bucket of sand, thereby enlarging my little "beach." I checked it out the other day for nostalgic reasons and there is no sign that it had ever existed. Of course, we really don't have any need for a walk-in entry point now that we have a ladder for the dock.

One of the fun things about having teenagers here was watching them together. Chris had a movie camera and he was always filming his sister in less than complementary poses, much to her chagrin. It sure would be fun to watch that movie now, twenty years later. One day, they dressed up for an "up north" photo. Jenny was wearing a pair of denim overalls and a red and black flannel shirt. She held a wood chopping ax. Chris put on an L.L. Bean rain jacket with a life vest over that, a fisherman's hat with lures, and he held a fishing rod in his hands. Somehow, his California style baggy shorts just didn't quite match the rest of the outfit. I love that photo!

Another thing I remember from that visit is that Chris really liked the pistachio fruit salad I made. It is just so much more fun to cook for company when they like your cooking!

As it turns out, 1997 was a good year to spend some precious time with our oldest grandchildren. Some big changes were about to happen in our lives.

SECTION 6

SPRINTING UPHILL

The teenager sprinted up the steep path from the dock and passed me like I was standing still. I was standing still. I was standing still and gasping for breath as I took one of several stops required for me to get from the dock to the top of the hill. That little scene took place during the summer of 1997. Rose and I had invited the youth group from church to a wiener roast to get acquainted with our two teenage grandchildren who were visiting from California.

We were at a stage in our lives when we could live our dream of having a house in the woods, living on a lake, sharing this beautiful place with friends and family, and all the wonderful creatures that lived with us. We had managed to live active and interesting lives despite Ray's growing limitations.

In 1998, we were settling into our Ely lifestyle. We were involved with LedgeRock Community Church (formerly Ely Baptist Church) and the North American Bear Center. Clearing the land and the building project had been therapeutic for me, however, my heart began to fail again. New drugs and treatments were being discovered almost daily but not quickly enough to help me. Doctors told me I had about two years to live.

As you can imagine, those were sobering bitter words and they took some time to digest. Somebody suggested a heart transplant and the next thing we knew, we had an appointment with Mayo Clinic. I made a list of questions to ask the transplant team and then did a pro-con list about what a heart transplant would mean for us. I sure didn't want Ray's life to be cut short by pursuing such a radical treatment. We did our medical research and examined our thoughts and feelings. Were we even up to this? We had a lot of questions to ask before we could sign up to go on the heart transplant list.

I was still hoping and praying for an alternative treatment right up to the very end of our long wait. We showed up for our consultation at Mayo and someone handed us a six-or eight-page printout of appointments.

Wait a minute!

"We haven't even decided if we are going to go for a transplant yet," I said as much to Julie, the wonderful professional coordinator we eventually got to know and trust.

Julie, sensitive girl that she is, quickly shoved the printout out of sight and told us the medical team would see us shortly.

"Please take a seat."

I was put through an exhaustive series of tests to determine if I was a good candidate for a heart transplant or some other method of dealing with my failing heart. The head of the transplant team was very knowledgeable and experienced. His calm demeanor and personality instilled confidence. He was sure they could help me.

We went through the interview process and were asked a myriad of questions about our life view. One of the questions was, "How do you go about solving problems?"

"First, we decide if the problem can be solved, then we make a plan to solve it," we said. "If it can't be changed, we try to learn to live with it."

We must have given the right answers.

After the evaluation, the doctor announced I was being added to the heart transplant list. I was given a pager and instructed to keep it with me 24/7. They also told me to purchase a cell phone, so I could be in touch with Mayo immediately if a heart should become available. Shortly after I received the pager, daughter Becky called. She told me Mayo Clinic had tried unsuccessfully to page me and was calling the additional phone numbers I had supplied. They had a heart which matched my blood and tissue type. Rose and I were stunned! So soon? I called Mayo.

Unfortunately, the donor's heart proved to be too small. My emotions went from relief to disappointment. Was I ready for this? I barely got off the phone when our neighbor, Ray, rushed in to tell us Mayo was trying to reach us. I am grateful for the caring neighbors we are blessed to have. We took advantage of this "false alarm" to resolve the problem with the pager and to think through our strategies when the "real" call came. It looked like this was really going to happen.

PREPARING FOR A LONG WAIT

For a summer that started early and ended late, 1998 sure passed quickly. Ice-out occurred on April 15, a month earlier

Ray building planters with bench

than last year. And ice-up still hadn't occurred as of December 8. To a true northerner, summer is measured between ice-out and ice-up, therefore, it had truly been a long summer. Why then, did it feel like the whole thing was just a blur, as if we had sped down the highway leaving summer in the dust?

Our year was packed with significant mileposts. Some events were of monumental importance and some were precious in their fleeting rarity. We had three family weddings that year and we got to be present at two of them. John and Val gave us a last-minute surprise by bringing my parents up to the lake for a visit. Mom and Dad would have been about eighty-three and ninety that year, and Dad was still taking long walks on his own. Then, seeing a furry pine marten peek at us through the dining room window was a treat for all of us. We finally glimpsed the otters that we suspected were occasionally hanging out under the dock. And we gazed at a sunset in six shades of orange.

The first big event was Chris' move to Mount Vernon, Washington, in early January. We spent Christmas at his home in Henry, Illinois, and helped him finish up some of the remodeling projects before his move.

Later that month, back home in Minnesota, Ray was listed as a candidate for a heart transplant. This was a mixed blessing; disappointing in that there were no other options and yet, a huge relief that Caterpillar insurance had agreed to pay for the procedure. Once we made the decision to have the surgery, we grabbed on to hope like a physical thing. But there were also things we wanted to accomplish while he was still able. There might not be another opportunity.

We decided it was important to fly out to Washington state to see Chris in his new home. While we were there, we took a couple of whale-watching excursions to see Orcas.

Between all our other events, we managed to get some brushing done in the woods, thanks to Becky and Seth and Frank and Mary Ann, friends who generously gave up their vacation time to do that. Brushing includes cleaning up fallen trees or limbs, as well as thinning balsam trees and brush that is a fire hazard if left untended. Amy and Julie were also great water girls that year and kept us supplied with cold drinks while we worked. They were nine and ten. The rest of the summer is pretty much a blur, except for a few rare canoe rides and swims in the lake, which we might not have taken time for if we hadn't had company. The thing about having company is we get to see our place through the eyes of our summer guests, as the vacation paradise that it is.

On July 4, 1999, around midday, straight-line winds hit the Ely area just after church let out. Ray's barbershop quartet planned to ride a float in the parade and do some singing. We were expecting Bruce to fly into Ely that day in a private plane, so after we had that surprise storm, I wanted to get home to stay by the phone. I was almost home when I came upon a tree which had fallen across Fernberg Road, blocking it. Someone in another car was waiting to get to town on the other side. I had my Jeep, so I turned around in the road, backed up to that fallen tree, got out my tow rope and hooked it onto the tree. In a couple of motions, I had the tree off the road.

The guy driving the other car came over to thank me. He shaded his eyes with his hands, trying to peer into the car. "If you people hadn't come along, I don't know what I would have done!"

Since there were no other people with me, it made me feel pretty puffed up. I was a real Northwoods woman!

We had made six separate trips to Rochester, Minnesota, where Ray was tested for every possible eventuality concerning his candidacy as a heart transplant recipient. They removed his gall bladder as a precautionary measure and installed a pacemaker/defibrillator because of an irregular heartbeat. During the October visit, when the device was interrogated, it was discovered that it had likely saved his life when it fired one time in September.

For the next two years, I was never far from a phone, always waiting for that possible call. The chances of receiving a heart transplant then were not good. In 1998, about 16,000 Americans could have benefited from a heart transplant. Only 2,340 transplants were performed in the United States that year. By 2000, an estimated 20,000 to 40,000 Americans could have benefited from a heart transplant. Clearly, the country has a bigger need for more organ donors.

We learned what we could about the transplant program—how it works, how recipients and donors are selected, about the surgery itself, and what we could expect before and afterward. The more we learned about the surgery and the drugs that would be a part of his life afterward, the queasier I felt about the whole idea. Even if the surgery was successful, keeping good health was going to take a concentrated effort and regular checkups in Rochester before and after the surgery. As the two-year anniversary on the waiting list approached, we could see that the doctor's prediction for life expectancy was proving to be very realistic.

There is nothing quite as likely to get your attention as being told you have two years to live. This news required a stop in mid-stride. Mid-every-thing. A total "about face." We were only sixty-three and sixty-one. That's still young! Right? When did we get this old?

COMPLICATIONS

In March 2000, life began to get more complicated. Ray was still on the waiting list for a heart transplant. We were told that the average wait was two years. We had just returned from a trip to Illinois to help settle my parents into a nursing home. Dad was ninety-one and in the early stages of Alzheimer's but was strong physically. He made a daring plan to escape one night and wore his pajamas on top of his regular clothes; then, after everyone quieted down for the evening, he walked out the door.

The nursing home was about twenty miles away from my parents' house, but I had no doubt Dad would have been able to find his way and possibly be able to walk that distance, given enough time. Thankfully, the nursing home had alarms activated on the door at night, so they stopped him. Mom was strong mentally but was needing some physical help. What a sad and difficult time this was! I was so thankful for my brother and sister, nephews and nieces, and Becky and her girls who helped care for Mom and Dad. We returned to Minnesota to try to deal with our own issues.

The week we got back to Minnesota, Ray passed out at quartet practice. His defibrillator fired five times, and he was taken to Duluth and stayed for observation for a week. Our closest neighbor was undergoing treatment for cancer at the time. Our kids and grandkids were all experiencing some huge changes in their lives. Two of our grandchildren had recently lost their mother and might need to come and live with us for a time. Have you ever noticed that the more things go wrong, the more things go wrong? There ought to be a word for that phenomenon.

After he was released from the hospital, Ray was having more shortness of breath and not able to do much work or anything else at this retirement paradise (work farm) that we called home.

I had carved and built several signs that were ready to be installed. One was the large carving of running wolves for the wolf center. The other sign, Rose's favorite, was the Boundary Waters Wash sign that I carved in the shape of an upside-down canoe. Wooden "clothing" hung under the canoe as if to dry. Thankfully, my friends Dave, Roger, and Dean were available and helped to install those signs.

SECTION
7

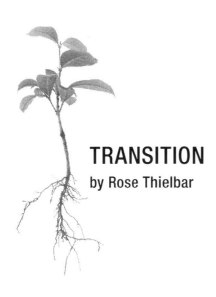

TRANSITION
by Rose Thielbar

Snowflakes descending on the wind,
Glissade in swift and repetitious waves;
Frantic with the effort to cover tender shoots
Exposed by yesterday's thaw.

Goose feathers, freshly plucked,
Come swirling, settling a downy comforter
Upon those impetuous daffodils and crocus.

It was the time of year when impatience reigns. Here in the north, we anxiously watched for fickle spring to finally settle in and settle down. A month before Easter, the weather was mild, snow had started melting off the roof, birds had already begun to flock back to the north country, and some misdirected daffodils had sprung up in front of the post office in town.

Encouraged, we scrutinized the spring catalogs and selected some new outfits for Easter, only to awaken on Sunday morning to freshly falling snow. The new outfits would have to wait. On Tuesday, April 6, we got another seven inches of snow. The new clothes were still in the closet. In Illinois, we would break out the white shoes and spring outfits for Easter service no matter what the weather. By then, we could see why Minnesota residents don't usually bother with Easter clothes. Sometimes, we are still wearing our mukluks to church on Easter.

Hope returned with warm sunshine the next day as we sunned on the south deck in our shirt-sleeves. We listened and watched as gulls checked out our lake looking for open water. Then we watched as they flew away, apparently not satisfied with what they encountered. By the next day, the snow was nearly gone. I found myself being lured into the garden with my spade. The spade made a thunking sound as it bounced off the frozen earth, so I put the spade away for a couple more weeks.

THAT "WASTE NO TIME" ATTITUDE

Those of you who know my husband will not be surprised by this, but to me, the faithful, supporting wife, it seemed just a bit foolhardy. One Saturday, in March 2000, on my birthday no less, Ray went with his barbershop quartet to sing in a quartet competition. He was not feeling well but insisted that he wanted to follow through on their plans to sing at the competition. Mayo had told him they wanted to hospitalize him and upgrade him to status one. That meant he would be in the hospital until he got a new heart. That made Ray even more determined to go to the quartet sing. The plan was to drive down to the Mayo Clinic together the morning after the competition. This "waste no time" attitude of Ray's reminds me of one of pastor's Sunday morning prayers. I shared with Ray's sister, Julie, about our pastor's pleadings with God about Ray's difficulty in dealing with "wasted" time and that he hoped Ray wouldn't have to wait long for a new heart.

"Your pastor sure has Ray's number, doesn't he!" Ray's sister said.

While we were packing for our trip to Mayo Clinic that night after the quartet competition, some of the ladies from our church drove out and surprised us with a quilt they had been working on for Ray. It was a beautiful creation with the bear paw design, and the colors matched our furniture and looked so good in our log cabin. The quilt ladies, other friends, and church members signed the back of it with their favorite

Quilt made by LedgeRock Quilters

Bible verses. We took the quilt with us to Mayo and it was a reminder of the love and support we experienced from our church family.

YOU WANNA MAKE A RUN FOR IT?

Our options had run out. I had begged God to find another way. But here we were in the waiting room at St. Mary's Hospital in Rochester, Minnesota. Ray—my best friend, fellow adventurer, husband, father of our children—had just checked in. In a few minutes, a hospital escort would come by to take us upstairs and settle him into a room.

We'd had several defining moments in our marriage but none quite so momentous as this. Ray could get a heart transplant and we would go back to our log cabin in the Northwoods, or there would not be a heart available and his heart would simply stop beating. I would go home to live out the rest of my days. Alone. Was I up for that? Living in a log cabin in the woods? I wasn't getting any younger.

He was only sixty-four, however, and still moving under his own steam. He could have months to live, or given how much God loves this man, maybe he could have a year or more. On the other hand, things could go badly in the operating room.

We could lose the few precious moments that remained to us. Trying to lighten the somber mood, I leaned over and whispered, "You wanna make a run for it?"

You gotta love this woman! As Rose and I sat in the admitting area, I think I was in a state of acceptance. The pain of angina had become such a constant companion that I was ready for whatever my future held.

OK. So, maybe I was the one with the somber mood: always weighing everything, imagining all the what-ifs. Ray was the one with the unshakable faith. As we sat there waiting, I was remembering all the rocky soil we had traversed to get to this point. We knew that there was still a long wait in front of us and all of the ordinary day to day tasks would still need to be done: paying bills, doing our taxes and finishing up tax returns for my clients, as well as doing membership and newsletters for the Bear Center. I would also need to keep in touch with friends and family. Those sorts of things would not take a timeout just because Ray was in the hospital.

After we got Ray settled into his hospital routine, I drove back to Ely to get my computer, bring some warm weather clothing, clean the refrigerator, and pick up the new license plates for our car. I didn't like leaving Ray alone in the hospital, so I was in a bit of a hurry to make good use of the time. I planned to get to Ely before the license bureau closed. I could have had them mailed, but if I picked them up in person, I might be able to get one of the license plates with the name of our town as a part of the number. There were a limited number of those still available. I had missed my turn in Minneapolis and was trying to make up for that on country roads. That's when I was pulled over for speeding. I had no trouble working up tears for the state patrolman, but I didn't give him my sob story. I tried to do what Dad had taught me and not make excuses.

I had kept most of the house rules, where I was staying, except for not having a computer in my room. I had to smuggle that in under cover of darkness. The thinking was that the residents of the house were all spouses of transplant patients and so it would be a good idea if we spent time encouraging each other rather than sitting alone in our rooms.

HEART TRANSPLANT

I arrived at the Mayo Clinic feeling really punk. Though I was not scared, I was concerned. I knew I had Rose and a lot of other troops praying for me. They wired me up and inserted tubes into me, making it difficult to get a good night's rest. That first night, I looked out my window and saw a tree. I learned later that my room was the only one on the floor that had a tree outside. About 9:00 p.m., I noticed a raven perched on a branch. Each time I woke during the night, that raven was still there. It flew away about 7:00 a.m. That night the raven returned to the same branch and left the next morning at the same time. The raven faithfully returned for seven nights. I was reminded of how Elijah, in the Old Testament, was fed by ravens. Was this a God thing? I certainly felt encouraged by the bird's persistence.

Also, unlike some of the other patients, I enjoyed the hospital food, even the veggie burgers. I sent thank-you notes back with the empty tray and arranged for a trip to visit the folks working in the kitchen. It was a fun experience and had its rewards. After that, every afternoon about 3:00 p.m., a nice lady would bring me an apple from the kitchen. Another food item I really enjoyed was dill pickles. Of course, dill pickles were a no-no because of the salt, however, I complained to the doctor about my wish for dill pickles.

He rolled his eyes and told the nurse to "give this man a dill pickle." He even wrote a doctor's order saying I could have one dill pickle per week. I made that pickle last for seven days. I had my own refrigerator, so I could have my pickle and my jar of salsa to put on the veggie burgers.

I was also interested in the helicopters and flight crew who had the responsibility of bringing donated organs to the Mayo Clinic. The ever-patient nurses helped arrange a visit to the helipad and flight crew personnel. What a joy that was!

Once the hospital legal department got word of Ray's outdoor tours, that was the end of that. This man of mine was going to have to settle down and act like a patient!

One morning in early May 2000, the transplant coordinator came and told me a heart was available and that I was on standby to receive it if they determined it was a good match and was healthy. I called Rose. A short while later, we were informed the heart went to another hospital, another patient.

Just a few days later, I was in Ray's room, waiting for him to return after undergoing another of the frequent heart catheterizations. Someone told me a nephrology (kidney) doctor would be stopping by. She wanted to warn us that there were some problems with Ray's kidneys and she didn't want him to be surprised. When Ray returned a few minutes later, he was still sore and tired from the procedure, but I did tell him that a kidney doctor would be stopping by. Doctors or technicians were always coming around, so we didn't think anything of it. But this time was different.

The nephrologist started to explain that Ray's kidneys had reached a low ebb of 29 percent output and at that rate, his kidneys would not sustain a heart transplant. Nor would his kidneys tolerate the drugs he would have to take to prevent rejection the rest of his life. Likely, he would require a kidney transplant in six to twelve months. Then she explained that a living blood relative would be the best kind of donor and that a success rate of 99-100 percent is expected in that case. We couldn't ask one of our children or Ray's sisters to give up a kidney, especially for a person as sick as he had become by this time. We also knew that any one of those blood relatives could also develop the Thielbar heart trouble and have need of both kidneys.

Then the doctor and her team began to describe the three methods of dialysis we could choose from. I began to cry silently while trying to keep a calm facial expression, so I would not upset the patient. I could imagine unplugging Ray from the IVs and taking him home for whatever time we might have left. All the while, I knew he probably wouldn't even make it to the car because his body was now dependent on the medication that was keeping his old heart going.

I watched Ray's face as he sorted through the information. I suspected that he was reaching the same conclusions I did. His situation seemed hopeless. He had come so far, and we had so much invested in this idea of a heart transplant. Doctors told us other organs could start to fail, and he would lose his eligibility as a heart recipient. We were devastated.

The doctor and her assistants left us, and we fell into each other's arms. I sobbed onto his chest, connected as it was with electrodes and IV tubes for the meds nurses were now administering directly into the Hickman. This was a port they had made in his chest rather than his arms and neck where he had developed infections. I sobbed, and my strong man cried, as well. The young nurse closed the door and left us for a time and then came back in and cried with us.

After we got through the shock, maybe an hour or so later, I don't know, we began to talk and to think through our options. We agreed that we could not ask a living person for a kidney. Then we thought about the patient upstairs on the sixth floor who, just three and a half weeks earlier, received three organs: a heart, a liver, and a kidney. His own failing liver had been donated to a woman who would have died without it. The woman who received the liver was currently at the transplant house recovering nicely, and nearly ready to go home. If this man could use a kidney from his heart donor, maybe Ray could, too.

After we came to this conclusion, the kidney doctor came back into the room and said she had conferred with the heart transplant people and they all agreed that in Ray's case, he could possibly receive both the heart and kidney from the same donor. Then we began to see that God already knew this problem would come up. Ray was not meant to get the heart that he had been on standby for recently. This way would be better.

It took us a couple of hours to work through this emotional trauma, with the help of my young Canadian nurse. I called her "Yup" because that is what she said all the time. I marveled at God's timing. Had I received the heart that was available a few days before, the decision regarding a kidney transplant would not have been made and I would have been facing a second surgery. Or worse. God was at work in all this. Yup.

Meanwhile, back at the facility where I was staying, the fire alarm went off about 12:28 a.m. It blared loudly, and a red light flashed. I doubt many could have slept through that. I pulled on my robe and stuck my head out into the hall as most of the other residents were doing. Since I was able-bodied, and this was the third floor, I told the others I would run down the three flights of stairs to see what was happening. Obviously, I wasn't the only person still up at that hour.

"It was me," a contrite woman said. "I burned my popcorn."

The firetruck came and firemen tramped through the house before they deemed us safe. I ran back upstairs to report to all the heads sticking out of all the doorways: "Burned popcorn." There were a bunch of sighs and slammed doors. Everybody went back to bed. I hadn't even been to bed yet.

I spent most of my daytime hours at the hospital with Ray. My evenings were so busy with paying bills, keeping up with my volunteer work for the Bear Center, answering emails, and doing my laundry that I seldom got to bed before midnight. The night before, I was still waiting for one of the clothes dryers at 11:30 p.m.

We had managed to keep positive attitudes through most of our long wait but we both knew that time was running out. I begged God to make another way. I struggled with this issue. What an extraordinary act of selflessness it was to be an organ donor! That anyone would even think to give their bodies to be used by others after their own lives were over was still a foreign idea to me. But, at the same time, it was so familiar. We knew the truth of God's plan that offered his son to die in our place. Now, somehow, this idea of a life for a life was made profoundly personal.

I finally accepted that transplantation was the only way to extend Ray's life, and if it did happen, we would feel indebted forever to strangers. What a humbling thought. I changed my driver's license at the first opportunity to reflect that I would be an organ donor. Somehow, signing an organ and tissue donor card made my mortality more real. I was so grateful that God was a part of my life, but at sixty-two, I still felt young. Thoughts about eternity seemed a long way off.

Ray was growing weaker. Friday and Saturday of Memorial Day weekend came and went. Sunday night arrived, and we still hadn't received a call. Here is a part of a letter I wrote to our dear friends, Phil and Beth that day when I was at my lowest. Phil was in the last stages of cancer, so I knew I didn't need to hold my feelings in. I could "tell it like it was."

"This has been a pretty down day for me. The big holiday weekend is nearly over, and our window of opportunity is slowly closing once again. Sorry about the morbid thoughts but I guess it goes with the territory. Even the transplant surgeon mentioned his disappointment this morning that we weren't having a warm and sunny holiday with all the inherent risks of outdoor activities that go along with it.

I'm trying to be content here at the transplant house, though the nighttime temperature in my room is eighty-four degrees. My room is on the east side, and breezes tend to come from the southwest, so opening a window doesn't help. There is no crosswind.

There are rules and signs posted all over the building. "The air conditioning is ON!" "No TV or computers in the rooms." There were rules about slamming doors, making your bed, wiping down the shower after every use, no dishes left in the sink, no eating in any room but the dining room, shoes had to be left at the door, no bare feet allowed, keep your own room clean enough for surprise tours, cook your own food, clean up the kitchen every time you use it, wipe out the washer/dryer after every use, sign in when arriving, sign out when leaving. I had one of those surprise tours one day. My computer was found out, and there were consequences! (I received phone calls several times a day to find out if I was tying up the phone line. Then they would hang up. These were the days when email was still new and misunderstood. I received a lecture about tying up the telephone lines with my computer even though I spent most of the day at the hospital. I tried to explain that I was using the phone less than people who made long phone calls. Months later, when we returned to Rochester for checkups, we found a whole new bank of computers had been installed in the family room for use by patients and caregivers. Finally.)

There are rules about the cupboards, the refrigerator, instructions about cleaning our own rooms, the laundry room, the kitchen, and stacking the clean silverware, handle side down. What? I remember this one because it didn't seem logical to me. We also had household assignments like garbage duty and washing dishes. Some of this is common courtesy and some just seems excessive. So far, I have received a note about complaining to the social worker about the heat, reprimanded for walking by without speaking, and received a threat that my car would be towed for having the wrong sized green permit on the dash. But other than that . . ."

Other than that, I was grateful to be able to stay there for $25 a night. That was wonderful! Looking back, I should have been way more grateful. Motels ran around $100 a night at the time. The other patients and caregivers were also wondrously brave and a great encouragement. We made some close friends that we have kept in contact with through the years. Sadly, three of our four closest friends have passed on.

That dismal evening, as I was getting ready for bed, Ray called. A heart was available! Could I come over right away? I hurriedly threw some clothes on, ran down the stairs, hugged the first and only person up at that time of night, telling this stranger that we had a heart and then I ran out the door.

It was after eleven o'clock and it was likely that surgery would be around 6:30 in the morning. I called Pastor Kevin and our friend, Roger, both of whom had made me promise to do so when the time came. The drive from Ely takes about seven or eight hours in good weather, but these two dear friends were determined to be there for us during the actual surgery. They called our church's prayer chain and started an all-night prayer meeting at the church. Those two guys managed to arrive about 6:20 a.m. that Memorial Day morning, minutes before surgery began. Roger pointed to his feet to show me he hadn't even taken time to put on socks.

The heart transplant was expected to take about twelve hours and the kidney would be transplanted after that. I was very thankful to have such good friends to keep me company. We waited in Ray's hospital room and prayed about the myriad concerns on our minds at that critical time. We got word that the heart surgery had begun, and not long after that, I heard the whomp, whomp of helicopter blades. Mayo One was descending onto the helipad. Pastor Kevin was praying aloud at the time, so I nudged Roger with my elbow and pointed to the sky. That helicopter was bringing Ray's new organs. It seemed a bit odd to me that they would start removing the old heart before the new one arrived. Just stop and think about that for a moment. What if something happened to the new heart? Or the helicopter? And, how would I, a simple farm girl, even anticipate the need to ask a question like that?

Hearing the helicopter arrive made me nervous and excited all at once. Maybe I would get to keep my husband and partner in adventure for a few more years. Maybe I wouldn't have to carry on alone. These emotions of hope and relief were mixed with the grief that I felt for some other family at some other hospital as they said goodbye to their loved one. I still tear up thinking about this eighteen years later.

While Ray was in surgery, the nurses began packing all of Ray's accumulated stuff and they asked us to begin moving only what he would need to the new room. It gave us something to do while we waited during the surgery. Roger took most of Ray's things to my car and then moved my car around to the parking deck for me. By then, we were told that Ray was taken off the heart and lung machine and his new heart was beating on its own. Now, they could start to implant the new kidney. He would have three kidneys for a short time and eventually, the two tired originals would stop working.

After much hugging, phone calls to friends and family, and more waiting, Ray was finally taken to his new room. It was isolated by walls and windows so that he would not be exposed to anything from the hospital environment. The nurses wore face masks, scrubbed before entering the room, and put on disposable gloves. Pastor Kevin, Roger and I could see Ray through the window of his isolation room and see that his skin had a new healthy pink color to it. He was hooked up to tubes and wires, but he looked wonderful. I got to scrub up, put on my mask, and go in and hold his hand for five minutes twice that evening. I was still dancing in the street on my way home to the transplant house and praising God that he had brought us this far.

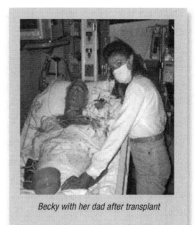

Becky with her dad after transplant

The next day, Ray got to stand at his bedside with a nurse on each side of him and do a half-dozen shallow knee bends. He was still attached to the breathing machine, so he couldn't talk yet. He was alert, and in keeping with his type A personality, he was trying to communicate something to me. I wondered what was so important. Something he forgot to turn off at home? Maybe he was in pain or something was pinching him. Was it a last request? Was the thing he wanted to tell me important instructions he forgot to mention before the operation? A change in our will? Was he trying to remind me that I needed to check the oil in the car? It could have been anything.

The next day, they removed his breathing tube, so he got to have JELL-O for lunch and a cherry vitamin slush for dinner. Since his throat tubes were gone, he could talk, and I finally found out what was so important that he wanted to tell me the day before. He wanted me to know that the clock on his wall had the wrong time. What?

Becky drove up from central Illinois the next day to be with us. We watched him through the window often that afternoon, not wanting to wake him. In the evening of the fourth day, Ray managed to take a baby step toward recovery when he shaved, brushed his teeth, helped with his own bath, and learned to record his first self-administered medications. He also sat up in his chair.

However, the day after that was disappointing to us because he had to have a pacemaker implanted. This was a surprise because the heart was a perfect match in every way and everything seemed to be going well. By noon, he was ready to have a few bites of his Cod Almandine with stewed tomatoes, some canned pears, chocolate milk, and a couple cans of Sprite. This was hugely encouraging, and his reports showed that the new kidney was working well.

I was looking forward to the day when he could come "home" with me to the transplant house. Things always go better when Ray is there. (Where does he get all his charm?) We expected to be at the transplant house until September.

The sixth day was difficult because they removed his IV pain meds. He was uncomfortable and developed a rash, and the nausea from his anti-rejection meds was back. They checked him for blood clots because he was complaining about shortness of breath. On paper, he looked good. I suspected that he was just wanting to race down the halls in competition with his buddy, Sue, next door, who had her transplant five days before Ray did. Sue had begun walking two days before Ray took his first post-transplant walk. We thought this was a good sign and meant that Ray was still the same ole' competitive guy we all knew and loved.

It was eleven days after his surgery when he had his first walk and that did us both a lot of good. Sue, of course, was an inspiration since she was a few days ahead of Ray. When she walked past Ray's window, she would wave and hold up two or three fingers, depending on how many trips she made around the nurse's station. Once Ray got to walk, it was an all-out competition. Sue would hold up a third or a fourth finger and then if she had done well, she would thumb her nose at Ray, egging him on. I often had chances to chat with Sue's husband, Larry, and his family, as we sat in the waiting room between visits with our spouses. What a tremendous blessing it was to have the friendship of these dear people who knew, so intimately, all the anxieties we were experiencing.

On the thirteenth day, the doctors let me take Ray home to the transplant house. He already had a 7:00 a.m. appointment for the next morning, so he would get precious little rest. He was tired but so happy just to get outside. That first day out of the hospital consisted of appointments from 7 a.m. to 6:10 p.m. Would we ever get to rest?

I received my new heart and kidney on Memorial Day, after two years on the waiting list and seventy days in the hospital. At the time, I was only the third Mayo Clinic patient to receive a heart and kidney at the same time, and I was the 188th person to receive a heart there. I needed time to adjust to living with a denervated heart, that is a heart that does not respond to an adrenalin rush or a burst of energy. If I rise from a chair too fast or take off running, it takes my new heart a while to catch up to the sudden increased demands for oxygenated blood.

I told Rose that with a new heart, I was going to be expensive to have around since, with a new lease on life, I wanted to upgrade my woodworking shop.

That sounded reasonable to me. I told him to go for it. I was often the beneficiary of his shop projects anyway. Ray had not only finished the cabin after it was closed in, completing the interior walls, plumbing and electrical, but he also built two bathroom vanities and several benches and deck chairs. He installed kitchen cupboards and appliances, as well. Of course, he also built signs for his business "The Woodbox." His new shop tools would get plenty of use.

We had lots of company at the transplant house after Ray was released from the hospital. Since we were spending the entire summer in Rochester, we had to leave our cabin unattended, which was a concern, especially during fire season. For this reason, we told friends and family that they were welcome to use it. We preferred to have someone there than to leave it totally unattended. We were grateful when they sent us reports, telling us our dream cabin was still in good shape and being used.

One day we got an email from our Northwoods neighbors, Phil and Beth, saying that they heard a lot of noise at our house. They said they weren't really worried since they didn't think thieves would be using the weed whacker and keeping the grass trimmed. It turned out that Chris was there doing some yard work, so we wouldn't find the place too overgrown when we got home.

For the first three months following my heart and kidney transplants, I remained on heavy doses of anti-rejection drugs that were toxic to the new kidney. A balancing act therefore follows as doctors adjusted drugs that would both fight rejection and not harm the kidney. I give the doctors credit for handling this with the utmost concern and with kid-glove treatment. One of the side effects of the anti-rejection drugs was a definite tremor in my right hand which made writing difficult. The first three months were the riskiest for rejection, but rejection is always a possibility for the rest of my life.

Upon arriving home, I had to avoid crowds where someone might be sick for a while because of my suppressed immune system. This, however, did not prevent me from singing with gusto at church. I looked forward to doing that.

Exercise was paramount as part of my lifestyle in so far as these powerful drugs attack muscle mass and bone density. We tried to walk as much as possible.

Ray had heart biopsies each Monday through the sixth week post-surgery. He had blood tests and x-rays on Mondays, Wednesdays, and Fridays unless there were changes that might indicate organ rejection. Changes might be flu-like symptoms, fever, sudden weight gain or loss, pain or tenderness over the transplant, variations in heart-rate or unusual fatigue. If there were any of these changes, tests were done daily. He had cardiac rehab on Tuesdays and Thursdays, as well as working out in the exercise room at the transplant house. After the sixth week, his doctors reduced his biopsies to every other week, then once a month. At the once a month stage, we would be able to go home. Ray was one of the few patients who never once experienced rejection.

On June 28, 2000, I wrote to friends—the ones I ranted to that day at the house, when I was at my lowest:

> "You asked how we are. We are great! We have been out taking drives, walks, errands, picnics, even going out to eat. Ray's appetite has returned, and the nausea is gone. He looks wonderful! He is doing very, very well; much better than I had ever dared to hope. We are walking the six blocks to his clinic appointments and back twice a day on non-biopsy days. Biopsies are done once a week now and will soon be every other week, then monthly. Chances are that we will still have to be here for ninety days after surgery, as they predicted. It takes that long to get the meds right. He still has a bit of a tremor in his right hand and doesn't sleep well but these things are improving little by little and not really a big deal. We usually go for a drive or "car shopping" on days when we don't have appointments. Today we went to Menards for a screwdriver."

We went car shopping a lot. I had to take the car in for repairs frequently, so it was time to trade it in. Every time we drove slowly through the numerous car dealerships in Rochester, a salesman would saunter out to see if we needed assistance. After a while, they recognized our car as being frequent shoppers, so they stopped coming out to greet us. We had one of those Ely license plates, where the name of our town is part of the license number, so that helped them know who we were. Those are the plates I was hurrying home to purchase when I got pulled over for speeding. Sometimes, after recognizing us as frequent shoppers, salesmen would wave at us as we cruised through their rows of cars.

One day, as our time in Rochester was ending, we drove through our favorite dealership and saw a different car in the used section. It was a dark purple Tahoe sport utility vehicle, which was exactly what we wanted and needed at that point. It would be big enough to haul my computer, printer, and mini-desk, plus all our accumulated possessions we had amassed after spending the entire summer in Rochester.

We had clothing for two seasons, the phone interrogator for his pacemaker, a whole passel of medications, and a few household items, plus two patio chairs we had purchased at Fleet Farm on one of our shopping expeditions. This SUV would be perfect! If we could just get a salesman to come out to talk to us, we would be that much closer to being able to go home to our log cabin.

SECTION
8

Chris, Noriyo, Bruce, Ray, Rei, Christopher and Jenny

OUR GROWN KIDS

Our kids turned out rather well, and we don't mind saying so. When Ray had his heart transplant on May 29, 2000, Bruce and Noriyo (Bruce's wife) were living in California. Bruce's kids were twenty, eighteen, and they had a two-month-old baby. Bruce, being the firstborn—the responsible type—was concerned for his dad's welfare, so he arranged to move to Minnesota to be closer in case we needed him. It was so wonderful to have him just a few hours away, ready, willing, and superbly able. He worked as a test pilot for an experimental aircraft company in Duluth. Noriyo worked at a hospital. They lived in Minnesota for several years. It was such a pleasure to be able to watch Rei grow up since we missed that with the first two grandkids while we were in Brazil. Our grandson, Rei, was born in 1999, before Ray's transplant. Chris was settled in a dream job near Seattle, Washington. Becky was married with two daughters and was working as an administrative secretary at Caterpillar.

Our kids have been a huge blessing to us all their lives. When they come to visit us at our Minnesota cabin, they come from as far away as California, Washington, and Illinois. They usually make it here at least once a year, and when they do come, it is almost always a working "vacation." Lucky for us, they inherited the hard work gene. Sometimes, we think they would rather work than play. It seems like there is always work that needs to be done: painting, repairing, cutting trees, and

Rei swimming at the dock

clearing brush at the cabin, plus all the awkward stuff like flipping mattresses, cleaning pine needles out of the eves, and helping us figure out how to use some of our newest electronic devices.

One year, our project was to put another coat of stain on the cabin and Bruce had planned to help with that enormous task. We bought enough stain to do one side and possibly a second side. We figured that was being optimistic since this was their family vacation. Bruce and Noriyo started the job by sealing all the windows with paper and tape. I noticed that he had evidently done this before because he was moving right along. I needed to run to the hardware store to pick up something. When I got there, someone told me Ray had called, and I was supposed to pick up more stain. Bruce had already painted one side of the cabin and was starting on the second side. He had brought his electric paint sprayer and planned to finish the entire cabin. I couldn't believe it.

We almost always have chainsaw work that needs to be

done, and the boys are always up for that. I usually try to get my bid in for a project before Ray's to-do list gets too long. If they are here in the spring or fall, the boys help carry houseplants outdoors for the summer or indoors for the winter.

We always hope to get in more swimming and canoeing during their summer visits. And we appreciate those who prefer to spend their days fishing for our annual fish fry. Seth, our son-in-law, as well as Jose, our grandson-in-law, usually catch most of the fish. Jose and Jenny have recently made us great-grandparents.

When Becky and Julie are here together, we can count on some lovingly simmered and seasoned pots of soup or other tasty dishes.

Becky usually drives the 640 miles up here to play the piano for the Thanksgathering program we have at our church. Winter visitors get to enjoy sledding on the hill, building a snowman out on the lake, or helping to decorate the Christmas tree.

Sometimes, we are headquarters for the launch of canoe trips into the Boundary Waters. Amy and Ted like to do that, and we still have all our canoe country maps from the years that we did our canoe trips. We are so thankful that we made those trips when we were still young. Amy and Ted are usually tasked with re-wrapping the insulation on the water supply pipe that runs from the lake into the house. Our granddaughter has plenty of practice in wrapping bandages since she is a nurse.

MOSES CAT

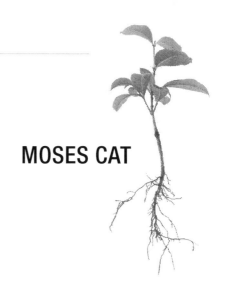

Ray was recovering nicely from his transplants and we were settling in at home after spending all summer at Mayo Clinic. All our kids were scheduled to come for Christmas and it was going to be a very special celebration. I had planned to make my legendary Swedish tea ring and a traditional Christmas dinner. I say "legendary" because Amy has taken over the family tradition of baking the Swedish tea ring.

Swedish Tea Ring

The house looked festive and we were planning to get a big tree to extend toward our cathedral ceiling. The only thing missing was a cat. We had always had a cat or a dog through the years and found them to be good company. Now that Ray was well again, we thought we could have a cat. We had kept our neighbors' cat several times while they traveled and that had worked out well. I had heard a message on WELY, our local radio station, that the vet had a yellow tom cat that needed a good home. Of all the cats we had through the years, my favorites were the yellow ones. I was considering this when I heard the announcement again. That yellow cat was still available. So, I drove to the vet clinic to check it out. I wasn't disappointed. I could tell by his face and eyes that he was a good cat. I brought

Moses cat and chipmunk

him home in a borrowed kitty tote on the front seat, trying to reassure him that everything would be alright. He seemed only slightly nervous, so I sang Christmas songs to him all the way home.

Moses had the most beautiful eyes and he had such a regal bearing, he reminded me of a king or a prince, as the lion in *The Lion King*. Our friend LouAnne, who was also our cat sitter, named him Moses and I thought it was a suitable and respectable name. Ray, however, just called him Cat.

This turned out to be one of our favorite Christmas celebrations. Ray was getting well, Chris was here, along with Bruce and Noriyo and their three, Jenny, Christopher and Rei. We cut a tree from our property that rose nearly to the top of our cathedral ceiling. We even had a cat to pounce on the decorations hanging on the tree. It doesn't get much better than this.

Once we came to understand each other, Moses turned out to be the best cat we ever had. I let him keep his claws since he would be a country cat. That was our first misunderstanding. He scratched my nice sofa. I told him how I felt about that. Eventually, he made his needs known and I bought him a scratch pole. None of our other cats had ever needed a scratch pole. I put this tool in his favorite spot in front of the patio door where the sun shines in. He always considered that his space. He liked to lie there in his little houseplant jungle and watch the squirrels and birds out the window. He was so happy with his scratch pole that he never scratched the sofa again.

There was only one other conflict we had to resolve and this one also had to do with his claws. When I sat in my recliner with a book or to watch a Netflix, he wanted to sit on my lap. He was a bit on the heavy side so when he stepped on my lap, I could feel his claws. He noticed that it hurt me, so he learned to wait until I pulled a blanket onto my lap before he climbed up.

One day, Moses was outdoors playing stalk the chipmunk while Ray and I were doing some indoor chores. I looked out the window and said "Oh, honey, look! There's a wolf outside." We were delighted to see the wolf until we remembered the cat was out there. So, I ran out onto the porch without my shoes and yelled at the wolf to go away. This was all a big bluff, since I couldn't do much barefooted, but I had to let the wolf know I intended to protect my kitty.

Just in case you are wondering, I should tell you that the chipmunks and squirrels were perfectly safe from Moses Cat. Even the squirrels knew that. And if kitty was out in the driveway, those squirrels would run circles around him just to harass him. If he was lying in his sunny spot in front of the windows, they would press their faces against the window pane and chant, "Nah, nah, nah, nah, nah, nah!" At least, I think that is what they were saying.

As soon as Moses saw me, he ran out from behind some hiding place and started to chase the wolf. The wolf trotted away, nonchalantly. If I hadn't stepped outside, would Moses have stayed in his hiding place? Was he trying to protect me? Or was he showing off for his humans? I wish I could have really understood him. He only talked with his eyes.

GUEST CABIN

In 2004, we were feeling the crunch of cramped space as our family continued to grow. Our kids were all married, and the grandkids were beginning to bring their friends and spouses.

Guest cabin

When the kids and grandkids came for a visit, a little extra space would be welcome. A young friend of ours in Ely had made a business of restoring old cabins so we checked out what he had and chose a cabin built in 1936, which happens to be the year that Ray was born. This cabin was still in its original spot at the YMCA Camp Warren on Half Moon Lake. The roof was missing but the logs were in good shape, except for one at ground level which would need to be replaced. It was a one-room cabin with a fireplace and a covered porch. The window cutouts were generous for that period and the original windows were, in fact, stored and available. The door was solid but had been used as a dart board, so we tossed the door and saved the wrought iron hinges and handle. Ray planned to build a new door with a stained-glass window that would include a great blue heron. The lovely fireplace could not be saved, so that would be another project for Ray who had already built two other fireplaces in his lifetime.

Dean, the seller, was responsible for numbering, disassembling, transporting, and overseeing the reconstruction of the cabin on-site. We would be responsible to prepare the site and provide all the necessary materials and labor for the job. This turned out to be one of the most enjoyable projects we ever initiated. We hired someone to build a road to the site about a city block from our main cabin. The logs were delivered in April, while there was still ice on the lake and the bugs hadn't yet emerged. It took Ray and

A little help from our friends, Chuck, Tom, Bruce, and Ray G.

me two weeks to sand all the logs with orbital sanders, making sure to preserve Dean's numbering so we would know where the logs were to be joined. Then Ray and Dean installed the footings, nailed down the subfloor, and laid the first course of logs.

We set a date for the log raising and put the word out to our numerous talented and able friends, not knowing who would show up. I had food simmering in crock pots, so I could be out there with my camera and not missing the excitement of watching the cabin go up. The day arrived, and we were thrilled by the turnout. I have photos of at least ten guys, counting Ray and Dean, who showed up. Most of their wives also came and brought casseroles or desserts. Some of our elder neighbors came with their lawn chairs to enjoy the excitement with us. I don't think I ever had so much fun as that day. Bruce and Chris were there to help, and Becky would be coming with her crew the next week.

The guys had thirteen courses of the fifteen-course log walls up by quitting time that first afternoon. The next day, they had the roof on and it was ready to shingle. Becky, Seth, Amy, and Julie brought a friend from their church and they all helped carry or install the shingles and did some site cleanup. Summer neighbors helped install the windows and Ray built the new door with a stained-glass window that he also created. I took photos of the project and made them into musical slideshows to document the restoration of the cabin.

After the log work and roof were completed, we were left with a gaping hole in the wall where the old fireplace had been. Family visitors and friends helped pick out rocks in anticipation of building the rock fireplace next year. We covered the hole with a piece of plywood for the winter. Bruce returned from Duluth a few days later with his spray painter and painted the entire guest cabin in a single day.

In the spring, I removed the plywood covering, anxious to begin erecting the stone fireplace. A steel double-walled fireplace insert had been delivered and, with Chris' help, we located and secured it in place.

Then we placed a cement block core around the insert and ceramic flue through the roof. After Chris left, I began the laborious task of choosing each rock and mortaring them in place, continuing through the summer months. I completed it in time for the first firing of the fireplace in early fall. Family members gathered as we enjoyed the aroma and sounds of hot dogs and marshmallows on wiener forks being roasted over the open fire.

I installed some basic electrical wiring that could be hooked to a generator or to the power grid at some point in the future. I built cabinets to Rose's design and laid black ash flooring. We chose ceramic tile for the porch floor which has turned out to be a huge success. We completed the "spiffy biffy" (outhouse) with a window, the same ceramic tile as we put on the porch, a magazine rack, and an artsy journal notebook for guests' reading and writing enjoyment.

The little cabin turned out very nicely and fit so well nestled in its spot overlooking the lake. We built a kitchenette and added a propane refrigerator and stove. We picked up the furnishings from visits to antique stores between Ely and Duluth. The guest cabin was just the right size for our grown grandchildren and their spouses. Early in the morning, the sun would drape its rays over that little cabin like a blessing.

THE NON-EVENT
THAT CHANGED OUR LIVES

Ray stepped out of bed one morning and one of his legs wouldn't support him. After we drove to the Ely Clinic, we were told to drive to St. Mary's Hospital, Duluth immediately. We hadn't planned on that, so we had to return home and get Ray's meds (and mine) and plan to be at the hospital for a few days. At the time, we thought this was just one more minor episode in the life of a man accustomed to experiencing multiple health events.

This turned out to be a much bigger deal than we had first thought. Ray had a DVT (deep vein thrombosis) which extended the length of his entire right leg, ankle to groin. While the surgeon was explaining that this was a serious condition, we were thinking it was nothing compared to what Ray had already been through. They removed the clot, but life did not return to normal. Ray's right leg has never entirely rid itself of the swelling, even after several years. Also, his left leg swelled, as well. A mesh device had to be inserted to keep clots from forming in Ray's lungs. And he needed to start taking a blood thinner called

Warfarin. Warfarin requires blood tests every other week and complicates any surgery or medical procedure because of the bleeding risk. Also, any bumps to his arms cause dark splotches. What we thought was probably a non-event, turned into a life-altering complication. Ray needed physical therapy and had to begin using a cane, as well as to begin wearing compression stockings.

In 2010, our once excellent health insurance was changed by Caterpillar. Ray's heart and kidney transplant had been covered, as well as all our meds, dental, and eye exams. Our extraordinary health care was what allowed Ray to retire early. The new policy was that the health insurance was cancelled, but Caterpillar would set aside funds for retirees to purchase health insurance, instead of providing that insurance. The new insurance that we purchased couldn't begin to match what was previously provided by the company. That's when we came face to face with the donut hole. Suddenly, all those very expensive, post-heart-transplant medicines were not automatically paid in full. At that point, we had to start paying for all dental and eye care, as well. While we had savings set aside for these kinds of things, this was a bit of a jolt to our financial peace.

I mentioned previously that we had a three-pronged goal to meet if we were going to live out our dream of building a cabin in the woods. We needed a car that would hold up for the long haul, good health, and good health insurance. The loss of health insurance was three for three. Living in our log cabin provided some wonderful experiences but it also brought a lot more challenges, work, and surprises than we could have ever imagined.

THE PAGAMI CREEK FIRE

This is the view we had as we drove home from town one day in 2001, during late summer. Ray captured this scene across Section 12 Lake. The fire started as a lightning strike in mid-August near Lake Two, which is about five miles away from our home. Officials were planning to let the fire progress naturally and even did some extra firing operations, hoping to keep the fire away from homes at the edge of the Superior Forest. A few days later, strong

Pagami Creek Fire

winds fanned the fire, causing it to spread sixteen miles in about an hour. Those numbers got my attention since it is about 16 miles to town and a round trip takes about an hour. Our house could be gone by the time we went for groceries and back.

This fire was reportedly ranked as the third largest in the history of Minnesota and eventually spread to almost 100,000 acres. Evacuations were ordered on the south and east edges of the fire. Hundreds of firefighters were in the Ely area for months. By late October, the blaze was only 91 percent contained. We were about a day away from evacuation when the wind changed again and blew the fire to the southeast. It traveled about twelve miles per hour that day. We drove up the old fire tower road six or eight times that week to see what the fire was doing. We watched airplanes as they dropped water and smoky red fire retardant at the northern edge of the burn. Near the end of October, 228 firefighters were still at the site, down from more than 700.

I had packed a bag of our clothes and had my mental list of what to grab if it looked like we would have to leave. That fire burned for three months, and the northern boundary was only four or five miles away, with only the narrow Kawishiwi River between us. Firefighters left in late October, saying the fire wasn't totally out and that it would take a good snowfall to finish it off. Thankfully, that is what eventually happened.

We attended a "Living with Fire" informational workshop at the local college to learn what we could about fire prevention. It was presented by USFS wildfire personnel, as well as some of our local first responders—the guys who drive the firetrucks. The most important thing we learned was by standing in front of one of Ely's new trucks. They are huge! There is no way one of those firetrucks could drive up our narrow, curving, hilly road. Our road is not only too narrow, but it doesn't have enough headroom for those gigantic trucks. A few of the local first responders were present for the workshop and said they would not even drive up a road that had no proper turnaround for the truck. Also, they certainly could not back up that far, especially if brush was hiding the backup mirrors. That means that we are on our own out here. I knew that from a little voice in my head, but this seminar brought it to the forefront. I guess we will just live like we always have: we trust in God, expect the best, but need to be prepared for anything.

CANOEING AMONG THE LOONS

My canoe glided quietly across the lake surface. The rhythmic dipping of my paddle made a soft swish to break the silence of early morning. The tendrils left by the canoe wake marked where I'd come from. Off in the distance, somewhere in the mist, was the sound I had been keenly listening for. The wail of a solitary loon split the morning solitude and reverberated

Canoeing with loons

across the water. The piercing echo bounced off the rocky shore. I gently tipped the paddle, directing the canoe toward the source of the call, while my eyes searched in the early light of a new day. I spotted a loon and two chicks. The mother occasionally dipped her head below the surface in search of small fish for her brood. As I drew nearer, the male surfaced with a minnow hanging from his beak. With a quiet mewing sound, the two chicks headed for dad and breakfast.

Finally, after a long winter snow, cold, and a frozen lake, I was back among my loony friends. Over the years, I have enjoyed the freedom of paddling among the loons. We established a rapport, allowing me to mingle up close with my camera. It was not always so. In my early encounters, I would have become impatient and approached too quickly. The loon, usually a male, would beat his wings against the water, throwing spray in all directions as if to say, "You're too close. Back off." He would emphasize that message by extending his neck, hissing, and bristling, thus making his image appear larger. I got the message.

The same loons must come back to the lake year after year. It is as if they expect me to show up. And when I do, they accept me and swim up to the canoe. I don't take this privilege lightly. The loons have rewarded me with wonderful memories that I cherish now that my canoeing is mostly a part of the past. Thank you, loons.

A MISSTEP

Christmas dinner 2014

It was the day after Christmas, 2014. The lace tablecloth was still on the table. Snow covered the landscape and we were feeling cozy and contented in our log cabin. The tree was still up, and we were basking in the warm memories of a family Christmas in the Northwoods. Yummy leftovers waited for us in the fridge. In fact, we had enough leftover food from Christmas dinner to keep us content for days. The kids were on their way home and would soon be boarding the airplane for their flight back to California.

I had already washed sheets and towels and we were almost ready to snuggle into our recliners to rest from the activities of the past few weeks. Ray had been putting things away in the garage loft when I heard him come back into the house.

He walked over to the downstairs sink. "Rose!"

"What?"

He didn't reply.

"Are you OK?"

"I don't know," he said after a weighty pause.

I ran down the steps and found him holding a paper towel to his face. He'd left a trail of blood from the front door to the sink and he was still bleeding profusely. I grabbed a chair, motioned him into it, and grabbed more paper towels. There was a gash on his nose with a flap of skin laid open, as well as a slim piece of earlobe that was missing. I lifted his hand to hold the towels in place over both wounds,

"Hold this. Don't wipe it. Don't rub it. Just hold it." He also had blood on the back of his head. I got a clean washcloth to clean his face a bit to see how badly he was hurt. Then, I dialed 911.

"What are you doing?" he asked. "You aren't calling the ambulance, are you?"

"Look at yourself!" I argued.

Thankfully, emergency personnel answered immediately. I described the wounds as Ray explained that he had fallen down the steps in the garage from about three-fourths of the way up, bounced off the wooden landing, and ended up on the cement floor. He had been carrying my AeroGarden (which has a glass covering over grow lights). It must have been the glass that cut his nose. This AeroGarden had been providing us with a taste of spring all winter long for several years. The fresh basil and thyme added just the right touch to homemade Italian soup. Unfortunately, we had only just started this year's crop. We had moved this electric grow garden to the garage, so the hum of the heat lamp and the light wouldn't keep our family members awake while they were here.

We had about twenty minutes to beat ourselves up over making such a decision before help arrived. Twenty minutes is long enough to examine all of the other things we had done, that we would do differently if we could have. Like, don't buy the shoes that were too large and a trip hazard, for instance. And don't try to do all of the cleanup in one evening.

We were thankful that one of the EMTs had worked out here at the neighbor's house during the summer and knew where we lived. He bandaged Ray's face and ear, helping to staunch the bleeding. Then he made a call to direct the ambulance driver who had gone to the wrong side of the lake (GPS isn't very reliable out here in the woods). Finally, the ambulance arrived, along with a policeman. While the ambulance personnel were getting Ray ready to transport, I escorted the policeman out to the scene of the accident. I hadn't been out there yet. Ray had left a trail of telltale red through the snow and in the garage where he had made a misstep on the stairs. You could see broken glass and tiny seedlings of basil and thyme which had newly sprouted a week or two earlier. The date of planting would be one of the things I would have done differently. Later. Much later.

Back in the house, I wiped up the blood as best I could, threw Ray's good winter coat in the washer, grabbed my purse, and hopped in the car to follow the ambulance. I tried to keep up but there was still snow on the passenger side of the windshield, so I had to stop, get out, and clean off the window. When I arrived at the hospital, I learned that Ray had lost both of his very expensive hearing aids at some point during the ordeal. Lynn, the emergency room nurse, bless her heart, was singing hymns to Ray as she cleaned him up. She suggested that I call a neighbor to go out and look for his hearing aids and the piece of his ear.

This was not a job for just any neighbor. Our closest neighbors, Bill and Kris, the ones who are always there for any of our emergencies, big or little, were traveling. Carol, our pioneer living-off-the-grid neighbor came to mind. I knew she would pray, and her capable daughter could do the driving through the deep snow out in the woods, in the dark of night. I watched as the emergency surgeon began stitching up Ray's nose. I could hear people out in the hospital hallway talking about taking the patient to Duluth by helicopter. His nose was broken, but remarkably, no other bones were damaged. However, there was some concern about a brain bleed, which could be life-threatening.

A cat scan showed a slight bleed on his brain, so they opted for the helicopter. By this time, dear Carol and Rebecca had arrived at the ER with both hearing aids and the piece of Ray's ear in a plastic baggie. God bless these women. Ray was on his way to Duluth for the first helicopter ride of his life and I was sent home to get our meds, clean clothes for both of us, and then I would drive to St. Mary's. I was glad I had the presence of mind to throw his coat in the washer while we waited for the ambulance. By now, his coat was clean, so I tossed it in the dryer while I grabbed meds and clothes. He would need this coat to wear home later. So far, he had always bounced back, so I expected it again this time.

Adrenalin kept me awake for the long drive to Duluth. Thankfully, I was familiar with parking at St. Mary's, but the entrance to the hospital from the parking deck was locked for the night. I used the wall phone for assistance and watched through the window as the guard across the street motioned for me to go back downstairs and use the emergency entrance across the street.

When I finally got to see Ray, his handsome face was swollen, scraped, and bandaged. He also had two very black eyes. The surgeon in Duluth tossed out Ray's piece of ear, saying that kind of tissue doesn't re-attach easily. Ray had a rather grim looking face for a few days. I took a photo for posterity. Our children didn't appreciate this. His face was very pale looking, kind of alien-like. If I had to try to describe him, I would say he looked like the grandpa of E.T. (Extra Terrestrial) might have looked had he been in the movie. Three weeks later, I snapped another photo, and Ray's regal face looked completely healed. Ray (spelled Rei) means king in Portuguese. My prince was already well again!

I sent emails to Bill and Kris, our closest neighbors, to give them a heads up about Ray's accident so they wouldn't be surprised when they saw him. And just in case they stopped by the house or garage before we got home, they wouldn't get the impression that a massacre had occurred. My quick clean up must have been adequate because they didn't notice anything out of the ordinary, other than Ray's computer was on and we weren't home. When they learned what had happened, Kris brought a bucket and some rags over to clean the garage steps where Ray had fallen. She took my throw rugs home with her to wash. I had swept up the broken glass but had not gotten back out there to clean up the stains on the wooden stairway where Ray had fallen. What a loving act! We are so blessed to have those two as year-round neighbors.

THAT SIX-LETTER WORD

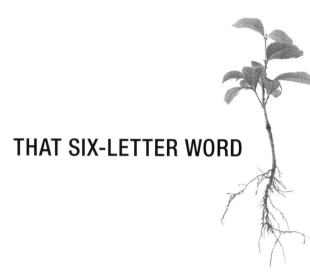

Not long after his heart and kidney transplant in 2000, Ray was told that if he lived long enough, he *would* get cancer. That may apply to almost anyone, but it certainly applies to patients who take immunosuppression drugs. Through the years, he has had numerous skin cancers removed, some from his nose, ear, mouth, near his eye, and other parts of his face. The surgeries were all successful. Then one day in mid-October 2015, he was scheduled for a regular colonoscopy here at the local clinic. Since Ray takes Warfarin because of the blood clot he had several years ago, doing a colonoscopy is a bit tricky and the INR (International Normalized Ratio) level must be below a certain number. The medical staff had some trouble getting the clotting factor to the right level, so they sent him to Duluth. An INR range of 1.1 or below is normal, a range of 2.0 to 3.0 is generally an effective therapeutic range for disorders such as a blood clot. The higher the number, the longer it takes to clot.

In January 2016, I was told by Essentia Health, Duluth Clinic that I had colon cancer. The tissues were sent to Mayo Clinic which is routine for me. They examined the tissues and confirmed that they were, in fact, cancer. I was told I would likely need to have a large part of my colon removed and would need to learn to deal with all that goes along with that surgery. Radiation and chemo were not an option for me. The other choice was to go home and let nature take its course. We considered the options and told our family what we were facing. Our kids and especially our daughter-in-law, Noriyo, were very vocal in telling us we did not have enough information. We needed another opinion. Noriyo is an x-ray technician and has seen patients who have had colon ostomies and have done very well. So, we went to Mayo and I had another colonoscopy.

We knew Ray would likely have to undergo a radical surgery. He had just completed his colonoscopy and we were in the outer waiting room at the Mayo Clinic awaiting news from the doctor about what they had found. This was turning into one of those days when everybody was running behind schedule. It looked like we would have a long wait to see the doctor, so I went over to the bank of computers and checked my email and Facebook accounts. I found a message on Facebook with a recording of songs done by the quartet Ray sang in while we lived in São Paulo, Brazil. This recording was sent from a young man we knew there. We hadn't heard from him for thirty-one years, but he had sent this recording of Ray and his quartet belting out one of his favorite songs. I turned up the sound and there was Ray's deep bass voice, along with the other three voices singing "Rise and Be Healed." I listened to the familiar words of this beloved song, one of Ray's favorites, about healing and peace through the name of Jesus.

My heart soared! *If God ever sent a timely message, this was it!* Hope is a wonderful thing!

I was still waiting to be called in to see the doctor with results from my colonoscopy when Rose called me over to the computer and played the song for me. I was moved to hear this recording we had made over thirty years ago. And to receive this message from Kolin just before we expected to hear bad news was something special. Kolin later told us he took that music from the CD with him as he traveled the world on his bike. He had rearranged the songs so that the "Rise and Be Healed" song came up first. A few minutes later, we were ushered into the doctor's office and told that they could not find any cancer.

We don't know how long this will last, and at this point, Ray has had eight colonoscopies in about a year and a half. What we do have is three months between procedures. So, every time he gets a clean bill of health, we know we have three more months of normalcy. Then every 3 months, they remove more new polyps and have them tested for cancer. It's a hassle, but we can do this. In a way, this just makes every day more precious than the one before.

THE BIG BLOWDOWN

When we went to bed Wednesday night nothing seemed amiss. There had been no severe weather warnings that we knew about. Later, a wind sprang up with the accompanying

Whole trees blown over in front of the cabin

thunder and lightning. The noise seemed excessive. I got up to see what was happening. This was between 2 and 3 am on July 21, 2016. As the lightning flashed, I could see that the trees on the north side of the house were bending over toward the ground. I was assuming they were bending back to an upright position as I had seen them do in other storms. The power had gone out, so I had to wait until the next lightning flash to see anything, at all. The wind was a loud roar, so I tried to stay away from the windows but wanted to see what was happening. I remember praying that God would protect our beautiful, almost new car.

Looking back, I wonder why I wasn't pleading for our lives. We are used to the way weather can change so quickly here, so we don't usually stew about the weather unless it is hot and humid.

I paused for a few minutes just to listen to the storm and I could feel the whole house shaking. This is a whole-log house made with large white pines and a few red pines in the ceiling. I had always felt safe in this house until that night. I would guess that the storm lasted maybe twenty minutes and then there was a lull until the wind started blowing again briefly. Finally, it was over. Ray always takes his hearing aids out at night, so he didn't even wake up. We seemed to be safe enough, so I let out a sigh of relief. I wouldn't have to wake up Ray. Without electrical power to see what had happened, I figured I might as well go back to bed.

The next morning, I expected to see some damage. Ray had gotten up at his usual time and was sitting in his spot on the living room couch, waiting for me to get up and join him.

As I started down the stairs, I heard Ray's deep voice call up to me. "Don't look out the windows," he said.

Of course, I had already looked out the windows. What I saw was far worse than I had imagined. I could see why I felt the ground was shaking during the storm. This house is built on ledge rock. When one of those two- to three-foot diameter trees in the yard fell on solid rock, it would have shaken the ground.

My favorite bigtooth aspen that grew beside the south deck, a beautiful old tree, had fallen. This is the tree that flying squirrels would launch from to get to the bird feeder after dark. Thankfully, this nice old tree missed the house. The white spruce on the west side had broken halfway up. I wouldn't miss that tree. We had been wanting to take it down because it was too close to the house and it was a fire hazard, but this would have required some professional help. The top half had fallen on the back steps, breaking a railing. We would still have to finish demolition on that tree and take down the rest of it. We went out on the porch but could not go any farther on the south side because of the strewn branches and tree trunks. Later, I counted ten fully mature red pines that had fallen over the picnic table south of the house. We could barely see the machine shed and the guest cabin through the blowdown on the east side.

When we ventured off the front deck on the north, we tried to assess the damage. A row of red pines on the lake side had blown over with their roots sticking up in the air. The car was in the driveway in its usual spot; trees were down all around it, but there wasn't a mark on the car. It also looked like the truck was unharmed, except for some leaves plastered to the back window. We would need to get a closer look. We had moved the tent camper around to the front of the house for the kids to use the following week. Thankfully, we had not set it up yet. A couple of twigs were on the camper, but it was amazingly unharmed.

We couldn't get to the garage without stepping over or under fallen trees. I had stocked up on meat and other food for our kids' planned visit, so we would need to start the generator to run the freezer. However, the generator was out at the guest cabin and we couldn't even walk through the jumble of fallen red pines to get out there. These pines, when mature, grow fifty to one hundred feet tall and were one of the most valuable parts of our property, for their beauty, shade, and fresh air scent.

We have always been a bit proud of ourselves for our self-reliance. The things we have accomplished together astound me, but this was not something the two of us could fix. The mile-long road out to the highway was strewn with trees and we could hear chainsaws running all over the vicinity. The power was out, and it looked like we wouldn't have it back for at least a week.

Our landscape was changed forever. I tried to make my usual priority list, but after a couple minutes of standing on the deck, we turned around and went back into the house and sat down. We couldn't go anywhere even if we had wanted to. Nature has a way of humbling a person. We had never felt this helpless.

We just sat there staring out the window for a few minutes, trying to figure out what had happened and what needed to happen. Getting the generator back to the house was going to be project number one. I couldn't just let all that meat, vegetables, and homemade baked goods go to waste. Maybe this is the thought that got my adrenaline flowing. Maybe I could find a route around the mess and pull the generator back to the house. Also, we needed to know if the guest cabin was still standing. I managed to work my way through, under, and around fallen trees, crawling on the ground at times on my tricky old knees.

The amount of work needed to clear this mess would be overwhelming. We were not physically capable and the cost to hire workers and heavy equipment for this task was more than we were willing to pay. There were over a hundred whole trees laying on the ground. This was one of those rare times when we were not able to get out of a predicament by our own strength.

Besides the cost, workers were going to be hard to get. This storm was widespread, and many people were in the same or similar situations. Good help was going to be in high demand for months or even years.

Trees were leaning against the roof of the guest cabin and they had ruffled up the edge of the shingles a bit, but otherwise, the cabin was not damaged. Whole trees and branches were laying in piles everywhere, and several trees were leaning precariously toward the guest cabin. They would have to be taken down. The storm had spared the generator but neither of us would be able to drag it through all that tangled mass. Normally, Ray moves the generator with the tractor, but I was willing to give it a try on my own.

Next, I made my way down our hill on the east side to check out the road. Maybe we could get to town to buy a second generator. Trees had fallen on both sides of our driveway and it looked like the mile-long stretch out to Fernberg Road was blocked. I couldn't walk any farther to the north or south on the road. We could hear chainsaws nearby. The newspaper later reported that we had experienced seventy to ninety mph straight-line winds. The damage covered several counties, so the electrical power would be out for days or longer. On the plus side, no large trees had fallen on the house, the car, the truck, or the camper. The house seemed fine, except for the south railing, where the spruce tree had fallen and the north railings, where the gas grill had bounced around in the wind, loosening the joints. The garage had a few small branches on the roof but was unharmed. Unbelievable! The buildings and our possessions were in amazingly good condition, given the magnitude of this storm.

Rose is a very special person. Her can-do attitude is one of her personality traits that has made it possible for us to survive in the Northwoods.

Meanwhile, our friends, Steve and Teresa, drove out to check on the storm and maybe pick some blueberries. Since they were out this way, they stopped by to check on us. The road crew had managed to clear the mile-long road into our place enough to allow traffic. Steve looked at the trees that were blocking my car.

"Is there any reason I shouldn't get out my chainsaw?" he asked.

I just smiled. You can't help but admire people who routinely carry chainsaws. Those dear people cleared a path for my car and kept going until the driveway was usable. Then they cleared the trees that had fallen on our motor boat, knocking it off the boat trailer. They even managed to get the boat and motor back on the trailer with the help of a come-along. I love Minnesota people. They treat natural disturbances like . . . well, natural.

Shanna, our beautiful cleaning girl, was scheduled to come that morning but was obviously not able to get to our cabin. She had her own mess of fallen trees. And she had farm animals that needed her attention. She managed to get out here with our friend, LouAnne, in the afternoon to see if we were OK. The storm damage covered our whole neighborhood, the entire road into town, and the surrounding townships. We learned from news articles that the storm extended north to International Falls and south to Duluth. It seems to have started just west of Ely and who knows how far it went past the end of the road on the east?

We managed to contact two of our other friends who lived outside the epicenter of the storm and they made it out to our property with their chainsaws later, that same afternoon. After several hours of labor, Dave and Andy had cleared a path big enough to fit the tractor through. That made it possible to bring the generator back to the house, so we could run the freezer and refrigerator. The food that I had prepared for our kids' visit would be saved. God has blessed us with the most amazing friends and neighbors. Bill, our year-round neighbor, and Steve, our friend from town, had just spent the better part of a day helping clear trees out of the road from a storm a week earlier. Other neighbors stopped by to check on us after they got their own roads opened. We ran the generator for a week before the power came back on.

Being a list-maker, I recorded all the fallen trees in the yard between the main house and the guest cabin, as well as the immediate area around the house. Maybe this would be useful for insurance or tax purposes. The trees weren't insured. Only the buildings were, but those were only slightly harmed, so we would likely not even have an insurance claim. I didn't count the trees that were leaning unless they threatened a structure. I ended up listing 103 large trees. I didn't even count the ones in the "woods" or at the bottom of the hill that were broken off halfway up and leaning into the road. Those would have to wait. We hired Sheldon, a former logger, who had the proper equipment to drag whole trees off the hillside and out of the forest onto level ground. Sheldon accomplished a lot in a few days.

All three of our kids and several friends had been planning to come for a dock rebuilding project. This had been scheduled the year before, well before the storm. So, when they arrived, instead of dock material neatly stacked and ready to be sawed up, they found over a hundred mature trees scattered on the ground looking like a giant game of "Pick Up Sticks." The dock project was postponed indefinitely. Bruce, Chris, Seth and their friend, Jack, along with Ray, all picked up chainsaws and started to try and make order out of chaos. The men trimmed the trees of their limbs and the girls, Becky, Julie and Gayle, tossed branches in the trucks and began hauling them away. They hauled forty-three pickup truck loads of treetops to the designated burn site. The burn sites filled up quickly, since all of the neighbors were also hauling trees from their properties. We ended up with a house-sized pile of brush out back between the house and the guest cabin. We put the best red pines aside to trade for some of the hauling work. Our family's three-day "vacation" was used up way too quickly and they all had to go home. Thankfully, Amy and Ted were scheduled to come a week later for their "vacation," so they also hauled brush. Our neighbor, Steve, not to be confused with Steve from town, helped to chisel down the size of the pile, little by little, through the rest of the summer. We ended up with four flat tires from driving over root spikes: one on the tractor, two on the plow truck, and one on Ray's pickup. Julie and Becky hauled the trees away while our friend, Gayle, spent the day filling in the large open-well-sized hole by the back steps where the aspen had stood. In addition to chainsaw work, Bruce reattached the railings on the deck, supervised the cleanup, and ran one of five chainsaws. Chris used his autobody expertise to bend dents out of the roof of the storage shed and "borrowed" dirt from my upper vegetable garden and brought that around to the house with the tractor, so we would be able to walk down the back stairs of the house. With that rather precious supply of garden soil missing, I suspected this was the end of the upper vegetable garden. We hired more work done around the property, and a year later, there is still an astounding amount of work to be completed.

We had to hire someone to de-limb the largest of the fallen trees. They moved the limbs to a spot out back at the edge of our yard. When the person we hired sawed off the tops of some of the fallen trees, the stumps, relieved of their weight, amusingly dropped back into their holes in the ground. We hired someone to haul some of the stumps away, but this opened a whole (hole) new problem. We had four large holes and shards of broken ledge rock at the front of the house.

ADJUSTING TO CHANGE

Last year's blowdown is still evident as we look around and see scars or stumps all around. It will be years before we can finish the cleanup. The fallen trees along the roadside will probably never be cleaned up since they are part of the Superior National Forest. Left to Mother Nature, the options would be decomposition or wildfire. I'm hoping for rain.

The morning sun hasn't risen over the tree line on our side of the lake yet, so the water looks dark in the shaded parts. Leaves have only just begun to grow. Looking across to the far shore, I can barely see the soft spring-green color coming on. A slight breeze ripples the water as it gently rolls toward the north end of the lake where it has an outlet.

Daytime temperatures have been in the 40s, 50s, or 60s. Perfect for cleaning up winter's untidy leavings. The bugs haven't come out yet, so that makes working outdoors easier. Birch trees are adorned with catkins; the leaves will come later. Newly emerged maple leaves have taken on that subtle rusty rose color that blends into an almost ocher green hue. Aspen leaves are ahead of the others and about half emerged by now. It's still quiet here at the lake. Most of the summer residents haven't arrived yet since nighttime temps can drop into the 20s.

Marsh marigolds should be in full force now, in mid-May, but are very scarce this year. I'm hoping that tomorrow's forecast for rain will provide the much-needed moisture.

I saw three gray jays this morning. Our pair must have had only one hatchling this year or the other one has already gone out on his own. The juvenile is the same size as his parents, but he is mostly charcoal colored instead of the typical charcoal and white you see in adults. Their gentle character makes them some of our favorite woodland neighbors. They have learned to trust us through the years and they flit from tree to tree, keeping us company as we walk in the woods or work in the yard. As the weather warms up, we will take our lunch to the open porch and they will come to us, expecting to share a crust of bread from our hands.

Our first hummingbirds have arrived but there is precious little in the way of natural food at this point. The only blooms at our house are the deep blue-violet Vinca. Ray put out the feeder as soon as we heard reports that the hummers were back. Some years, those dainty little birds will buzz up to the window where we sit at our table, hover there, looking in on us to remind us that they have arrived. Obviously, some of these birds have been here in previous years. Our human neighbors agree. Those hummers know exactly where we hang the feeder.

Who can resist those imploring, hungry little hummers? I sure can't. It has become my job to mix up the sweet water and fill the feeder. Late in the summer, I may have to add another feeder because it seems like they consume twice the amount of food in the days before they begin flying south.

I look out the window by my desk as a new sound gets my attention. It's the buzz of a chainsaw. Ray is out there cutting up the fallen trees that I pointed out to him yesterday. I really wasn't hinting. I was asking if maybe we should hire somebody to clean up more of the blow-down. I don't want him out there doing that kind of work these days. He uses a cane now because of unsteadiness on his feet. There is scarce flat ground for walking up here on this rocky hill.

A Northwoods man really needs his chainsaw. I bought one with spring assist starting which allows me to operate it. Now, let me at those trees my bride wants removed. Yeah!

The next day, as we drove to town, we checked the swampy spots along the road for marsh marigolds. Only a few were blooming here and there. Then while we were in town, rain arrived from the west. It was a gentle but steady shower. By the time we had completed our town chores, we noticed on the drive home that there were dozens of bright yellow marsh marigolds that had opened in those few hours. Also, the tender new leaves of aspen, dripping with rain, are so much greener today. The photographer's word for this is "saturation." How appropriate.

Now that we have had our first rain and things have greened up, the post-storm landscape doesn't look quite so hopeless. However, the sight of fallen trees on both sides of Fernberg Road on the way home from town remind us of the huge fire hazard we have out here. This is our only road out.

We have adjusted somewhat to the changes made by last year's storm. We miss those big trees, but we can see the lake better now. We can even see the tiny island from the window over the kitchen sink, making for a little distraction from the task of washing dishes. Thankfully, there are still enough red pines between the lake and the top of the hill to preserve the woodsy feeling. There is more open space and that makes it just a bit safer from fire and wind. We still need to do a tremendous amount of work, but on the plus side, little sprouts of woodsy shrubs are coming up and covering some of the scars in the landscape.

GREEN BEANS AND PETUNIAS

My vegetable garden gets smaller every year. It is partly my knees that tell me to do that and partly the critters that eat the vegetables. I don't mind sharing, but I don't appreciate wastefulness. Why would a chipmunk take one bite out of every tomato instead of finishing off one or two whole ones? We've learned to put the tomatoes in chicken wire cages which will allow us to eat some of the fruit of my labors. Deer eat the tender new leaves of green beans, so now I plant the beans in pots up on the deck.

Last week, we took a one-day vacation down to the North Shore, then went on to Duluth for some shopping. When we got home, I found that some critter had eaten the purple petunias in my favorite loon-shaped planter that Ray had built. They had looked so nice. I like to mix pink and purple. It just seems like a lovely combination against the black and white backdrop of the loon. I wasn't too upset; after all, the critters called this place home way before we came along. And I could imagine how tempting a purple blossom would be to a bunny. I was pretty sure it wasn't a deer that walked up the staircase. Surely, those big snowshoe hares don't come up on the decks, but anything is possible. The last time we had a large hare crop, there were numerous large cat sightings reported on the EFN (Ely Field Naturalists) mailings. People in the area have reported seeing the occasional lynx, bobcat, and rarely, a cougar. Ray was privileged to see a bobcat on the way home one day. The critters who live here with us are one of the most interesting aspects of living in the woods.

Later, I walked around to the south deck where I keep the bean pots. I had four pots of newly sprouted green beans and one pot of cucumbers there when we left on our mini-vacation. Now, all the bean leaves and cucumber leaves were nibbled off. The beans will recover and eventually yield a nice crop if the stems aren't cut too short. So, Ray has made some new chicken wire cages for the beans, as well as the tomatoes that grow in the ground. It is hard to keep ahead of those wily critters. One time, I saw an almost ripe tomato in the garden and thought it would be perfect the next day. Of course, some critter took a large bite out of it before I got there. I was still blaming the snowshoe hare that we had seen earlier. Until the next morning.

We were enjoying our usual, early morning practice of sitting on the sofa that looks out to the backyard one day when Ray spoke up.

"Oh, what was that? It just ran past your compost heap!"

When I got up to go to the other window, I saw it. The sun had just rounded the tops of the trees to light up my flower garden out there on the south side. She was kind of golden, like things look when the sunlight is just right. Golden, cream, brown, and black, blended into a chubby very healthy groundhog. I wished my camera had been downstairs, but I didn't want this behavior to continue so I had to tap on the window and run out on the porch. It looked so cute! This lovely specimen of woodchuck was daintily pulling a tall stock of lupine over and nibbling off the blue blossoms right in the center of my flower garden in full daylight.

I shouted and clapped my hands until she ran over the hill. I knew it was a temporary fix. But the mystery of who ate the petunias and the green bean leaves was solved. More chicken wire fixed that problem.

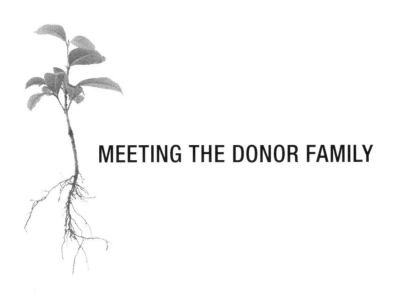

MEETING THE DONOR FAMILY

At Christmastime 2016, Ray got a call from the LifeSource Transplant Network asking for permission to be contacted by the organ donor family. We were about to celebrate our sixtieth wedding anniversary and Ray's eighty-first birthday. We were coming up on the seventeenth anniversary of the transplants. Twenty years earlier, we never could have imagined that we would be able to reach those milestones. We had written to the young widow of Ray's organ donor, Steve, that first year and received a letter in return, but we sensed that it was just too painful to correspond so soon after her loss. Now, seventeen years later, we were invited to exchange letters with the young man's grandparents, mother, and sister.

In June 2017, we finally met the grandparents of Ray's organ donor and found them to be kind and loving people. We arranged to meet them at our church one Sunday after they drove up to Ely from north of the Twin Cities. Through them, we learned more about this family and the incredible young man whose life and death made such an impact on our lives. We knew that Steve was a twenty-three-year-old policeman who was healthy and living a remarkable life of service to his community. He loved helping people and took part in numerous charity events and services. We were privileged to read some of the newspaper articles about him following his death. His grandmother was very generous in sharing some of those things with us.

"He was always the first one to line up to help out . . ." one police officer said in the article.

"You just knew this kid was going to do something with his life . . ." another said.

They commended him for his honesty, fairness, professionalism, and sense of humor.

"He always had a little glint in his eye and gave a slight head nod to indicate he was joking about something . . ."

Steve's sister, Melissa, who was slightly less than a year older, has written several heartwarming, yet amusing accounts about her brother, helping us to get to know him just a little bit.

"He had an amazing sense of humor! One day I was on my way home from work and there was a cop behind me with flashing lights, so of course I panic and pull over and when I looked in the rearview mirror, the cop was gone. I told Steve the story when I got home, my heart still pounding, and he laughed at me and said he loves doing that to people. I told him it wasn't funny."

Melissa wrote letters describing how she learned about her brother's accident. She had driven home from work, taking a different route than was usual for her. If she had taken the usual route, she would have come upon the scene of the accident.

When she got home, she called their mom, as was her habit. While they were on the phone, the other line kept buzzing. Here is her account:

"I clicked over, and the guy introduced himself, stating his name, followed by 'State Patrol.'"

I paused and listened. He said he had Steve at Regions.

"That's OK. He used to work there," I said.

"No, he's in the ER."

"OK, he's got friends all over the hospital."

He paused again. "He's been in an accident. He's in the ER."

"OK, I'll come up and get him."

He paused again. Of course, it's starting to sink in.

"Ok, I have my mom on the other line. I'll tell her to meet me there."

I was the first one at the ER, and they handed me his badge and a couple of other things. I don't remember. I handed them to my mom right away when she got there. For some reason, it felt like I was holding his life in my hands, and it was really hers to hold. He was in surgery when we got there. We sat in a waiting room forever, it seemed, before they got him stable and to a room.

They moved us up to another waiting room, but we couldn't see him yet. They told us about his injuries. They wouldn't give us any sort of prognosis. We could go see him, but we had to stay quiet. He could hear us. He had tears in his eyes when we would talk to him. He would squeeze our hands; his beautiful, blue eyes never opened for us again . . ."

"When we walked into Steve's room to sit with him, the nurses were laying him back down in bed. His nurse said he

had stood at the end of his bed. They told him he was heavily sedated and needed to lie down. I kind of giggled because no one could ever really get him to listen. He did his own thing.

I went into Steve's room again on another day. He had a cone-shaped thing on his head. It measured the pressure in his head. We weren't allowed to talk to him or touch him anymore. They didn't want him to get stimulated and have the pressure go up. We were supposed to watch for a certain number on the monitor. It the monitor displayed that number, it would mean more brain damage. The numbers just got higher and higher the more swelling he had. This was the start of us realizing this was the end.

One day, the doctor came to talk to us in the waiting room. He said the swelling wasn't going down. At this point, Steve didn't have any brain activity. It felt like a ton of bricks fell on us. The waiting room grew extremely quiet. The doctor asked if we knew what Steve's wishes were since the ventilator was doing the breathing for him. That's when I remembered the conversation that we had a week before his accident. We hadn't talked about organ donation, but thankfully, it was on his driver's license."

Just the week before his accident, I came home and told him the story of a patient who was very young. She had just graduated from nursing school and ended up in a diabetic coma, on a ventilator, on tube feedings before going brain dead. The ventilator was pretty much keeping her alive. Her mom was there every day, despite the doctors telling her she would never wake up. She never wanted to take her daughter off life support. She believed she would wake up. It was heartbreaking to watch. When I told Steve about this patient, he shook his head.

"I would never want to be on tube feeding, and if I were ever on a ventilator, just pull the plug. I don't want to live that way," he said.

I went into his room one last time. I looked out the window. It was extremely gray and cloudy and just dreary. I stayed with him, held his hand, and told him I loved him. The clouds broke, the sun shone through the clouds, and it was the most beautiful golden yellow. The streaks went right over him. It was amazingly peaceful. I couldn't cry anymore. All I could do was stare at it and at him. I thought the doctors had it all wrong. This was a sign he would be OK. That he would come back to us. As I look back and think about it, I think that's really when he passed away and his soul left us. He wasn't hurting anymore. He was at peace. And I was there to witness it.

"At the service, police officers and firefighters from all over showed up to pay their respects. Two Lino Lakes officers stood on either side of him while people came up to view him. When nobody was up there, I looked at the officers and said, "Thank you. Please make sure he doesn't go anywhere." I said it before I could even think, and the look of horror they gave me before they smiled was priceless. If anybody knew Steve, they knew his sense of humor. I think that's when I knew I had to keep that part of him alive. Laughter has gotten our family through a lot of tough times.

When we reach the burial site, I knew this was it—the end of letting him go physically. Pastor Linda starts talking and only gets about three words in when a very happy bird started chirping loudly. She paused and waited for him to stop. After she started again, the bird interrupted her a second time. Then it happened a third time. All we could do was laugh at the defeated look on her face. She started laughing, too.

Later, Ray and I heard from Steve's mother, Fay. She described the same scene that Melissa had seen with the light across Steve's bed on a very cloudy day. The accident that took his life happened when the motorcycle he was riding was struck by a car at an intersection. We have a few pictures of this young man. His handsome face has a huge smile. I think we would have enjoyed knowing this very special young man. I'm so glad we have heaven to look forward to. Someday, maybe we can all meet in the heavenly realms and enjoy a bit of adventure exploring together—all of us—in our new bodies.

Melissa told us how much she enjoys road trips, so we invited her and her mother to drive up and spend a day with us in Ely. We spent a very enjoyable day showing them where we live, having lunch together and visiting the North American Bear Center. It was like meeting some long, lost relatives for the first time. The hugs were heartfelt on both sides. We embraced them in gratitude and humility and they embraced us as though we were extensions of their son and brother as a part of him lives on in Ray.

A YEAR AFTER THE BLOWDOWN

It is interesting how nature copes with loss. It just keeps on keeping on. A year after the blowdown, we have grown accustomed to having fewer tall trees around us. It is fascinating to watch how nature handles this. The large aspen that used to be located south of the house sent up dozens of little aspen shoots. Wild roses and asters are coming up at the edge of the hill on the south side where the red pines grew before the storm. On the north, between the house and the garage, there used to be a cluster of balsam that was nice because it hid the ladders that hang on the garage wall. Now, the ladders and the garbage cans are fully visible. Nature is going to need a little help with this spot. I am still waiting for inspiration about what to do with that disturbed ground.

In winter, the evergreens were so picture perfect when they had snow in their boughs. They were the highlight of homemade Christmas cards for more than one year. A lovely mountain ash tree at the edge of the stand of balsams managed to survive the storm. We were always thinking we should encourage it by thinning out some of those thick growing balsams. The ash tree has interesting compound leaves and red berries that show up in late summer. The birds like them, too. Now, a year later, the balsams have "gone with the wind." The ash is now thriving as the only tree still standing at that spot.

Where there was shade last summer, we have more light, and the juneberry tree and the clump of paper birch appear to have grown much taller. The shade garden has been overcome by grass now that it is open to the light. Sometimes, I am rueful of the day we planted grass. I do love how the freshly cut green grass accentuates the flowers in my numerous rock gardens. This year, with the abundant rain, the grass grows faster than we can cut it.

The juneberry tree continues to be a source of delight. Those sweeter-than-blueberries red fruits will be ripe soon and turn to a dark almost purple color. They look like miniature apples about the size of a large pea and have a bit of a pithy texture with tiny seeds. Birds and animals alike are attracted to this tree, which grows wild here. Red squirrels are already sampling the fruit, even though it isn't fully ripe. This tree offers such an abundance of fruit—enough that there might be enough for both man and beast. We like to choose the choicest fruit from the low branches and pop them into our mouths. And I like to use a handful of these berries along with wild blueberries in pie. If any raspberries are present, I can add those and have a triple berry pie.

In winter, the juneberry tree is filled with birds which vary somewhat every year. This past year, we had the large and noisy blue jays in abundance, as well as a good number of pine grosbeaks. The pine grosbeaks, with their thick dark bills, vary more than other grosbeaks in their coloring from pinkish red to gold or russet. Some years, we tend to get large flocks of evening grosbeaks in their golden plumage, and rarely, we'll see rose-breasted grosbeaks. Occasionally, we'll spot a ruffed grouse or two perched in the tree. Large numbers of black-capped chickadees, along with nuthatches and various woodpeckers show up every year.

Early spring brings a variety of warblers and other birds as they make their way further north. In the summer, ruby-throated hummingbirds make their appearance and ravens stay all year. We had rain showers almost daily in the spring of 2017 and on into early summer. The trees, shrubs, and grass enjoyed a growth spurt, but we saw fewer blooming flowers. We only saw four hummingbirds this spring, compared to the usual twenty or so.

I planted a new flower garden at a spot off the driveway where we lost so many red pines. When the stumps were removed, we were left with empty holes and chunks of ledge rock standing on edge, sharp side up. Originally, I planted creeping phlox on a naturally curved rocky berm, but the berm and the plantings were destroyed. It was impossible to walk there on one of the prime viewing spots on the property, so I had a small load of dirt hauled in and tried to recreate the rocky berm. Then I added some ferns and flowers. I tried to curb the expense by taking diggings of plants from around the yard and woods. I used ferns, yarrow, Vinca, iris, columbine, golden moneywort, a few unknowns, and some yellow flowering sedum (stonecrop) which I had to buy.

Feeling very blessed, I accepted the offer of mulch from Bill and Kris who claimed to have an overabundance of that good weed blocker. Later, we hired someone to grind some of the storm-felled trees with a chipper, and Ray brought a dozen tractor bucket loads of chips to add around the edges. It is looking pretty good now, except for where some four-footed garden-lover nibbled a few flowers and hostas.

Rose used the tractor to move the largest of the upturned rocks, saving some to place on top of the berm. Then she ordered a load of dirt and moved that around, so she could match the vision she had of how the berm garden would look. I'm proud to call that tractor driver my wife. Rose calls the tractor her "big wheelbarrow."

Carrying dirt with the tractor bucket is a lot easier than pushing a wheelbarrow. Since I can't use the tractor to pull weeds and grass, I've gotten a bit behind in my work on the yard and gardens. We've had to make a few changes to accommodate our aging bodies.

Rose with her big whellbarrow

SECTION
9

Shovel Point in background, Lake Superior

OUR MINI-VACATION

We took a half day vacation one day and drove down to the north shore of Lake Superior. We had been busy trying to catch up on mowing and outdoor chores between spring showers. The black flies and mosquitoes were bugging us so much that we were often chased back into the house to escape their torment. All our other obligations and everyday responsibilities and concerns were taking a toll on our energy. We figured that a change of scenery would be a good thing.

The first glimpse of Lake Superior as we drive Route 1 never fails to inspire. The immensity of this great cold-water lake is still a thrill. It reminds me of driving west and seeing our first glimpse of mountains, still many hours distant. I thought about the mountains while we walked some of the easier trails at Tettegouche State Park and the Temperance River. I admired the native plants around the visitor center and entertained the notion of using more native plants from our property. A lot of local plants would be ideal if they weren't so difficult to dig and so few and far between. I like the dwarf dogwood, bunch berry, and the vine-like twinflowers. Joe Pye weed blooms pink later in the summer. Native plants would be less costly and more long-lasting, if only I still had the energy I had when we moved to the Northwoods.

In years past, we enjoyed hiking the waterfall trails on the North Shore and have walked most of them. One year, we hiked as many as we could in two days. My favorite is the Cascade River Trail, where the hike is mostly on even ground and with every bend in the path, a new waterfall comes into view.

On this trip to Tettegouche, Ray had his cane and I opted to leave my walking stick in the car since I was carrying two cameras. We strolled along, always stepping off the side of the path so younger walkers could pass us. When we came to steps without a railing, we turned around and took a different, less ambitious path.

I remembered when we didn't have to look for easier paths. We used to look up at the mountains in Glacier National Park in Montana and know we were going to walk to the top. And after we walked to the top, our view was a broad sweep down mountain sides, across lakes and sky, with trees as far as our young eyes could see.

We walked around a section of the ridge trail, so we could come back down a different path around the mountain. Confident. Able. The trip the day before to the north shore was a reality check for me. In my spirit, I'm still that girl who looked at the mountain and knew she could climb it.

I wrote a poem about our hike out to Shovel Point at this state park twenty-one years ago. It just seems appropriate that I include it here. The words are so much more a reality now than they were then.

THE SITTING TREE

by Rose Thielbar

The Great Lake rages in the storms
and hurls its waves upon the shore.
Some who venture out endure
and live to try it yet again.

Tireless in its endless motion
surges, pauses, like a heartbeat,
pulsing in eternal rhythm,
powered by the unseen forces.

The sitting tree
Photo by Ben Tower (Ray's nephew)

The waves, like years, erode and tear
and leave their mark upon the land.
Men and trees alike, send roots down
to a place where we can stand.

While walking on the shore one day,
I spied a tree not seen before.
A cedar with its twisted roots,
grows high along the shore.

Frayed by his circuit round the sun,
Old Cedar saw much in his time.
If he could tell us and we'd listen,
speak volumes by his mere existence.

Children spring upon the pathway,
the icy spray invigorates.
Scarcely see what they have trampled,
too much alive to know life's worth.

The oldsters soak up summer sun
while gazing into wintry depths.
Notice how the sunlight flickers!
See what lies on the trail ahead.

The lake, when fair, seems sanctuary,
sunlight skipping on the waves,
lulls the spirit of her watchers.
Cheers and comforts, mesmerizes.

Worn by time, my steps more plodding,
I pause to let my breath recover.
Though briefly, not to grant admittance
to the thing that age has done.

I pause, and for a moment,
halts the brutal march of time,
as I savor now the present,
feel more tranquil and aware.

Old Cedar, weary, resting,
wisely leans on what's at hand.
A boulder just beside it,
Cedar sits. He does not stand.

SUMMER'S END

My husband informed me this morning that today would be three minutes shorter than yesterday. That is a bit depressing since it feels like summer only just began about three weeks ago. I didn't really need to be told because I can see out the window that summer is beginning to taxi to the west-facing runway. Warblers are already on their way farther south and the ruby-throated hummingbirds have begun their preflight refueling frenzy. This must have happened while we were busy entertaining summer guests. I had noticed that the Shasta daisies have lost their perky blooms and gone to seed. I woke up an hour later this morning since this is the first day I have had in over a month when I had no pressing reason to rise early. The day is overcast and cool and just lends itself to a slow idle. A person needs a day like this from time to time.

Tonight, we took our stroll around the square here on the property. It's sort of a country block where we can walk without trying to do the steep hill of the driveway. We take our walking sticks now that we have learned how devastating a fall can be. We walked out to the guest cabin, admiring the blooming weeds that seem to have escaped from the septic mound. It was a road mix that includes wildflowers, some of them quite appealing. Birch leaves are beginning to turn yellow and last night's wind sent a few to the ground. Two of the red osier dogwood shrubs are sporting dark red leaves. So is the Carolina creeper.

We admired Ray's job of weed whacking behind the little cabin. This is the first time we have had to cut weeds there. Until last July, large red pines stood in that spot. I trimmed the clump birch yesterday and Ray cut out three juneberry trees that had some mysterious disorder that curled up the leaves and turned them black. It took two tractor bucket loads to haul it all out to the burn pile. This is where our old white pine used to be before last year's blowdown. Now, it is rock rubble with piles of brush that will have to wait until snow falls before we can burn them.

When we got to the guest cabin, we stopped and sat on the porch. It offered a nice view of the lake just before sunset. We watched a red squirrel as it leaped from limb to limb in the top of the Norway pines far above our heads. This squirrel paused long enough to scold us just because that is what he does. He was busy harvesting pine cones and we watched and listened as the dropping cones plunked two or three times on lower branches as they fell toward the ground.

The lake was so beautiful tonight, quiet and peaceful. A young couple took their wave runner out for a spin, made a round and turned down toward the east portion where it ends up in what they call the Ink Spots. Another couple brought their motorboat back home to our side of the lake. They probably had dinner with the neighbors.

We had to drive to the Mayo Clinic again last week for another colonoscopy. We try to do what we can to make that trip a getaway vacation. We were trying out our new GPS for a real vacation trip we hope to take in September if the Mayo reports are good. We named our former GPS Prudence since she usually gave us good advice. Prudence got on our nerves sometimes, though, because she was a bit of a nag. "Turn right. Turn Left." Then she would lose her cool if we took a wrong turn and would say in a complaining voice: "Recalculating." We were so happy when the new GPS had a different voice. This one is so much more tolerant. So, it just seemed right to name this one Patience.

I must have typed in some misinformation at first try because Patience told us to go to Rochester by way of Duluth. That was clearly wrong. At least she was patient about the whole thing. I had to figure out the quirks of using the new device, and finally, Patience and I got it right. Maybe I forgot to check the "shortest route" option. Usually, on our Mayo Clinic trips, we can look forward to eating out at a nice restaurant. Unless Ray has been instructed to fast. Then it isn't a vacation, it's simply a medical trip. The good news this time made the whole experience worthwhile. Ray is cancer free!

OUR FALL GETAWAY

Since the Mayo Clinic report was excellent, we decided to try our fall getaway trip in which we drive around Lake Superior. Never mind all the work that needed to be done around the cabin. Our annual Thanksgathering celebration was coming up and Ray had a program and special music to plan. I had

Sturgeon River at Canyon Falls

slideshows to create. Then, Christmas would be sailing in right after that. However, it just seemed like we should celebrate this timeout from medical appointments. Instead of having to go to checkups every three months, the clinic told us we could stretch it to five months the next time.

We started our drive around Lake Superior going counter-clockwise since we had already done quite a lot of exploring on the north shore, all the way to Fort William at Thunder Bay. Our passports were freshly renewed, so we were good to go. Our first stop was Bayfield, Wisconsin. We took a boat trip around the Apostle Islands. The weather was hot and muggy, but we chose the upper deck of the tour boat in favor of better photo ops. The islands had such interesting outlines, shaped by wind and water. If we ever get to return, we will take a shallower boat to check out the sea caves, as well. Rain was forecast for the next day and I had the beginnings of a sore throat, so we decided to spend the rainy day in the car and started toward Pictured Rocks National Lakeshore. The next day was expected to be nicer.

Mossy overhang

The highlight of this trip turned out to be Canyon Falls, which is about midway between the Apostle Islands and Pictured Rocks. I had seen a few photos that made it seem like an interesting place to explore. We looked at the trailhead and I wondered if I was up to it. I asked a young twosome who were just returning to the parking lot, "What is the trail like for a couple of oldies?" Thankfully, they were positive we could do it. It was an easy hike, they said, probably less than a mile, along a very interesting stream called the "Sturgeon River."

The water was shallow, so I doubted any self-respecting sturgeon had swum there in recent history. The stream bed was large slabs of rock that the water flowed over in descending levels. It was so lovely and peaceful. The canyon, from which the place gets its name, began at the falls and made for exceptional photo opportunities. The rock wall opposite the falls had an overhang of vibrant green moss arranged as only nature can accomplish in an understated way, untouched by human hands or feet. Farther downstream, the water made an abrupt left turn in front of a higher rock wall. This one resembled a ruined stone building with a door and windows that would have been fun to explore back when my knees were a decade or two younger. The site even has a rock slab "step" placed just in front of the quasi "door." Did Mother Nature do that or a creative person? This is a shady secluded spot that beckons the imagination to take a journey of its own

Our main destination for the trip was Pictured Rocks National Lakeshore. This required another boat trip. We signed up for that and awakened the next day to very foggy weather. We walked down the pier, arriving an hour early, as had been suggested for those who wanted the better vantage points on the tour boat for photographing the scenes. The boat trip takes about three hours, but before we got to the first point of interest, the fog had thickened. Once we got aboard, we were not able to see anything beyond the edge of the boat, only that thick, white fog.

The pilot told us the boat was made of fiberglass and he pointed out shallow areas of the lake. He then began to entertain us with shipwreck stories from the days before GPS and depth finders. It was truly a relief when they told us we were going back to the dock. We would get a full refund in case we wanted to try again the next day.

The next day, we went an hour early and waited in line again. Happily, the fog had cleared by the time we got out of the harbor. We were impressed with the areas where the rock walls were streaked with minerals. What appeared mostly black to our eyes took on strong colors of blue, yellow, orange, and white after some post-processing of our digital pictures. As interesting as this was, it was the huge battleship rocks and the shapes carved by nature that were most captivating. If we ever tried it again, we would try harder to find the one scene we found on a website while researching the area. It contained an interesting waterfall that spilled directly into the lake from a short elevation of just a few feet. The water washed over sandstone where it had etched permanent ripples on the surface of the rock. We're not positive, but we think we know where that spot is. I suspect we might need to do some hiking to get there, or at least find a shallower boat to get to that spot. Maybe next time.

Once we got around the north side of the lake and started to head south, it seemed that our car sensed we were on the trail toward home and started to pick up speed. We still had more places we wanted to explore, like Slate Islands which were formed by a meteor and are home to a herd of caribou. It would be fun to learn about that if my knees hadn't hurt quite so much, and if it wasn't raining, and if I didn't have a cold. We crossed the border back into the US with mixed feelings. We were cutting the trip short by a few days, but we had a couple of stops we hoped to make on the North Shore. One of those was High Falls. We had done that hike once, maybe four or five years earlier.

OUR HIKE TO HIGH FALLS

We got our signals crossed before we even started the hike to High Falls. I headed for the trail and Ray said, "Oh, I thought we were going to the visitor center first."

"Do you want to go to the visitor center?"

"No, I'll just go back to the car and get my cane. You go ahead. I'll catch up with you."

I unhurriedly walked a few yards and decided it might be a good idea to go back to the car and get *my* walking stick, too. I tried to get his attention to let him know I was going to the car, but he didn't see me waving my arms. Nor could he hear my

High Falls, MN

restrained shouts. Or that I was trying to jump up and down, thinking the motion would grab his attention. By the time I got my stick, he was already well on his way up the trail. I picked up my pace, trying to catch him. Every time I rounded a bend in the trail, I could see him up ahead, ready to go around another curve. I hollered with the most lady-like voice I could summon every time I got a glimpse of his back. He was moving along at an unbelievably fast clip. His habitual limp, a result of the DVT a few years ago, was hardly noticeable. I couldn't believe the speed at which this eighty-one-year-old heart recipient moved up the winding trail. I didn't want him to overdo anything unnecessarily. Obviously, Ray thought I had gone on up the trail ahead of him, as he had suggested, so he was trying to catch up with me.

I imagined him getting to the viewing platform and seeing that I was not there. He might think I had gone on up to the top of the falls. That would be significantly farther and more of a climb. Would he decide to bushwhack his way after the trail ends? I could just see him perched up there with his camera at the edge of the falls where the water hurls itself over the cliff. Other hikers were traveling at varying speeds, so I tried to be discreet in my yelling to get his attention while trying to increase my velocity. So, there we were, me trying to catch up with him, trying to catch up with me.

This faster pace was getting the best of me. My knees were rebelling, and I was breathing like I had run uphill for about a mile and a half. Which is pretty much what I did. Finally, I reached the end of the trail and climbed the last of the steps. There he was, totally absorbed in photographing the beautiful scenery of the High Falls. Something about his absorption and calm enjoyment ticked me off.

"You sure do walk fast for an old guy with a walking stick and it is high time we get those worthless hearing aids checked!"

The other hikers just smiled and commented on the impressive view.

"It sure is tranquil, isn't it!" someone said.

A MYSTERIOUS TRANSIENT EVENT

Our trip around Lake Superior was a wonderful, enjoyable trip, but it did point out to me that maybe I should have *my* health checked out, especially my knees. I planned to do some research on knee replacements and talk to some of my friends about their experiences. Then, just four days later, I was resting in my reading chair, trying to get over the cold and cough that I caught on vacation when Ray came in. He had been at the neighbor's house, shutting down their cabin for the winter.

He came halfway up the stairs and said in that hesitant way that I have come to dread, "Rose . . ." he paused. "I think I must have fallen."

I met him at the top of the stairs. He had a scrape on his hand and a little blood on his face. I looked him over and decided we had better get his coat off. His left arm, the one attached to his already dislocated left shoulder, had been severely scraped. (We were about to have that shoulder repaired when the doctor told us he had colon cancer, so the

360

shoulder repair had to wait.) The skin on his arm was already compromised because of the deep bruises caused by his blood thinner. I checked his clothing, looking for mud to see where he might be injured. The only mud was on one knee, as we might expect since he was shutting off the water supply.

His arm was bleeding a lot, thanks to the blood thinner. His coat and shirt were soaked, so I threw those in the wash, grabbed a clean shirt for him, and drove him to the clinic. They took some x-rays and found that his arm was not broken but there was a bone in his face that was cracked. I reminded them that he had a fall a year or two earlier and broke his nose, so they rechecked. This was a new break. They bandaged him up and told us to come back the next day for a bandage change. We had to go back twice a week until he was mostly healed.

The next day, we went to the scene of the accident to try to reconstruct what had transpired the day before. He doesn't remember what happened. We retraced his steps and saw where he had kneeled at the water shutoff valve outside the cabin. The only clue we found was his flashlight laying on the ground near a stump and a mud puddle farther down the path. I couldn't imagine that he had fallen there because his clothes were not that muddy. But that's where we found the flashlight. Apparently, he was able to finish up his work and put his tools in the truck before he drove home. The doctor had a name for this kind of behavior (transient global amnesia) and said that it was not unusual for someone to fall and manage to get home without remembering the events.

I don't want to give the impression that this man is accident-prone. Nothing could be farther from the truth. He is supremely competent, able to leap tall buildings. Well, no, not that. But if you want to see a project pursued to the finish, Ray is your man.

AGING IN PLACE

Every day, it seems like we have some new reason to doubt the wisdom of our decision to "age in place." We don't want to leave our place in the woods. My self-care mode has always been "if you ignore it, it will probably go away." Ray's health has been another story, as you've probably guessed by now. This man I couldn't catch on the hike to High Falls was eighty-one, but his heart was only forty. Besides

Rayn and Rose, 60th Wedding Anniversary
Photo by Beth Gustafson

that, he has always had a young attitude. He still turns ladies' heads. My heart was seventy-nine at the time and I think my knees must be way older than the rest of me. I had a fall on icy steps several years ago, hurting my hip.

This took about a year, plus three visits to a physical therapist before I fully recovered.

"I think you want to be stronger than you are," the therapist said.

Well, yeah.

After the hike to High Falls, I visited my doctor and had some x-rays taken. I learned that I have osteoporosis and my knees are bone on bone. I got cortisone shots and the news that I will likely need to have my knees replaced at some point. Maybe. Eventually. We'll see.

In the fall of 2017, Rei, our youngest grandson, started college. Then in November, our first great-grandchild, Atreyu, was born in California. These days, change seems to have become the new normal.

We had to swallow our pride this fall and spend some money on repairs because we just aren't what we used to be! One of those repairs was to have the posts replaced on our porch and deck railings. Ants and moisture had caused the posts to be unsafe, so we called our friends, Bill and Barb, that dynamic duo from up the Echo Trail. They came out and did the work for us. It is hard to believe that our log cabin is thirty years old.

The next project seemed like an extravagance and a bit on the side of high-living. We had an automatic generator installed. Pulling the old generator out of the garage is becoming a little more difficult with every power outage. And once we get it out, we have to drag the long cable over to the house, stepping through snow piles (which can get up to waist deep) at the edge of the path. Next, we go into the house with our best flashlight and flip the electricity off. Then we make our way around the outside of the house to the basement door, trekking through the taller-than-the-car stack of snow that the plow has pushed up at the edge of the driveway. Under the porch, we duck our head, walk like a duck to the half door, then take the perilous steps into the dark crawl space/basement. Next, we locate the under-the-house canyon and carefully maneuver unyielding rock to the power switch. Finally, we flip the power over from house power to generator power. A lot can go wrong in that process when the power is out, and you can't see where you are stepping.

While an automatic generator seemed extravagant when we installed it, our first snow that came in the middle of the night, cutting off the electric power, proved otherwise. The furnace shut down in mid-cycle and all our little electronic lights and the digital clock went dark. The snow was heavy with moisture. The heavy snow must have knocked a tree down on a power line somewhere. Power could have been out for hours. Before we took our next breath, we heard the sweet sound of the generator come on. That new extravagant purchase began to hum, sounding like a lullaby. We didn't even have to get out of bed.

A DAY IN THE LIFE

I was a bit hesitant when Rose asked me to share what a day in my life looks like. The question is: well, which day?

"Write about yesterday," she said.

I chose to comply, thinking someone who reads this may find encouragement that an older man lacking eight days of turning eighty-two can still get outside and do stuff.

Yesterday was a Tuesday in January 2018. It was −16 degrees at 6:30 a.m. when I got up, with a forecasted high of 10 degrees. I placed my hearing aids in my ears, trudged to the coffee maker, flipped it on, and checked the outdoor thermometer: −15 degrees. Did I really want to go to Bible study? It would take me a while to conclude that I did want to go.

While the coffee maker was happily perking, I dressed and shaved. I took my meds, washed down some hot coffee, and gathered the makings for oatmeal. While it was heating, I put bird food in the feeder. I often wonder how those birds can consume so much.

The computer monitor was staring at me with a blank expression on its face, so I turned it on. While it was booting up (where did they come up with that expression, booting up?), I headed for the shop to stoke the wood burning stove with wood. I notice in passing that my pile of firewood is slowly disappearing and wonder how long it will last.

After breakfast, I checked for emails including prayer chain requests, as well as other church business. As moderator of the church board, there is always church business to attend to. I planned my morning to allow some sit-down time with my wife between my first and second cups of coffee. Time has proven that my sit-down time with Rose pretty well determines how my day goes. Most days start with me finishing a cup of coffee on the couch while waiting for her to descend the stairs.

"Good morning, sweetheart," I say. "I love you."

She always smiles. "I love you, too."

We sit on the couch and plan our day.

Anticipating a new snowfall (and the resulting difficulty of navigating our road) I plugged in the engine heater and tried starting our old 1995 Chevy plow truck. All I got for my efforts was a grunt from the motor. Dead battery! Since the truck was buried under a foot of snow from previous snowfalls, I had to clear off the snow from the hood, so I could hook up the battery charger. I lack upper body strength and my left shoulder is nearly useless. I wondered with some trepidation if I had enough strength to lift the hood. To make matters more daunting, I was standing in a foot of snow. Deprived of solid footing, I managed to raise the hood enough to hook up the charger. Snow was beginning to fall so I lowered the hood enough to shelter the battery charger and chose to let the battery charge overnight, keeping the block heater plugged in. Maybe tomorrow.

We were out of the house by 8:30 a.m., headed for Bible study. I like to be there and have coffee made for those who arrive early while Rose gets water on for those who prefer tea. Flurries were still coming down. We made it down our hill in fine shape, but coming home would be a different story. Forget trying the plow truck again tomorrow. I needed to plow today. I just hoped it would start when we got back home.

By the time we completed chores in town and had lunch, it was 2:00 p.m. On my way out to the truck, I stopped to put more wood in the wood stove. Once again, I slowly hefted the hood up and unhooked the battery charger. I found the driver's side door frozen shut and had to use a flat bar to open it. Putting the key in the ignition, I turned it to start the motor. Glory be, the motor started. I was elated. Putting the transmission in drive, I headed down our hill, plowing as I went. At the bottom, I noticed something was wrong. The right rear tire was flat. How am I ever going to get the truck back up the hill to repair the tire? Maybe I should just let the truck sit and call Phil, the guy who plows our frontage road, and turn all the plowing over to him. Of course, it would be costly, but my tiring body was becoming more in favor of that option. I prayed, "Lord, let me get this truck back up the hill and help me inflate the tire and finish the plowing. In Jesus' name."

Repeating that prayer over and over, I turned the truck around and drove up the hill. All the while, the flat tire was letting me know it was rebelling. I parked the truck near the garage door, started the air compressor and, hoping the tire was not off the rim, proceeded to inflate the tire. Now, if only something else does not go wrong. That old truck and I finished plowing. By the time I hauled in more firewood, I was tired but encouraged. We got the job done. I did not have to call Phil the plow guy after all. Maybe another day.

THIS MORNING'S VISITORS

This morning, Ray and I were enjoying our usual early morning time together, sitting on the couch and enjoying the snowy scenery. Some days, we spend five minutes, and other days we spend up to forty minutes. The forty-minute buzzer of the washing machine is our signal that we have things to do and had better get on with it.

Some movement across the backyard caught our attention. "Oh! It's a pine marten," I enthused. The marten stood up to get a better view of anything that might be available for a snack. I hadn't carried out the compost bucket yet since we had about six inches of slushy snow overnight. Also, we had not yet put up the bird feeder. This first snow caught us by surprise. We were still trying to decide about whether we would put up the feeder. Sunflower seeds can get very expensive after word gets around to all our bird and animal neighbors. Also, the task of putting up the feeder isn't an easy one. Ray and I have been ordered by friends, family, and our doctors to avoid falling. Shoveling paths is one thing, wading through deep snow on uneven ground is something different.

This marten seemed to be smaller and younger than the last one that came to visit. From this distance, his luxurious coat looked all brown. It was just beautiful. I quietly got up and started to look for some scrap of food.

"The gray jays are here, too," Ray whispered.

I found some lunch meat which had been malingering in the fridge just a tad too long, so I grabbed a handful of that and quietly opened the porch door. When I opened the door, a deer ran off down the trail on the other side of the house and three gray jays flew to the porch railing. I left three separate offerings for the jays on the railing and walked around to the south deck, hoping that the pine marten was still nearby.

There he was, heading back toward the woods, so I whistled like you whistle for a dog. My whistle sounds more like *phewt, phewt* than a real whistle, but it did the trick. He turned around and stood; his long body on those short back legs, watching me. I held up my hand with a dangling piece of meat and he saw it, so I tossed it to the top of the porch stairs in plain view. He hesitated, not fully trusting me, so I gave him some space and went back into the house. I peered out from behind the curtains to watch. He started back toward the house and just then a gray jay spied the meat that I had tossed out for the marten.

"Oh, no. The gray is going to get it."

The jays had already taken the tidbits that I had given them. The gray jay started for the meat but saw the marten approaching, so it turned in midair and flew to the birch tree, instead. That was just enough time for the marten to run up the snow-covered steps and claim his treat. I expected him to grab it and scamper away, but he stayed right there on the deck until he had eaten all of it in tiny little bites. What a delightful way to start our day. If we did the sensible thing and moved to the city, we would never see these kinds of things!

DRIVING HOME IN A WHITEOUT

The forecast was for six to twelve inches of snow on Sunday morning. Ray took the truck in to church an hour early since he had a board meeting to lead. I drove the Equinox in later, on our nicely snow-packed road. The sky was gray and overcast but no snow was falling.

Just three and a half hours later, we learned that five more inches had fallen. We wanted to go straight home, but I had a long grocery list and we needed a few staple items because it might be a week before we got back into town. By the time I got to my car, I had an inch of snow on my bare head. I tried to shake it off as I had seen our dog Sam do years ago. I must have added a new layer of snow on my scramble into the store a few minutes later because people would look at me and smile. Their amusement level seemed to be heightened to more than the usual "Minnesota Nice."

Ray decided to follow me to the store, then we could make the drive home together in our separate vehicles. Just in case.

I hurriedly picked up only the most important items, anxious to get back on the road before it became impassable.

Once I was done, Ray wanted me to go first so he could follow. By this time, it was snowing so hard we could only see about two car lengths in front of us. I thought I saw Ray back his truck out of his parking spot at the store and start to follow me, but when I got to the east end of town, two cars were behind me, but neither vehicle was Ray's. So, I pulled off and waited. I couldn't identify the cars in these conditions until they were directly across from me. Eventually, he arrived. I didn't want to just pull out in front of him, so he ended up driving the Fernberg ahead of me. I didn't think he knew that I was behind him. This episode reminded me of our hike to High Falls. We didn't have cell phones yet. And after we had cell phones, we weren't used to plugging them in every night or having to turn them on the next morning.

My windshield wipers were going full blast and I had difficulty finding Ray's truck ahead of me. A stream of white blew out from behind him, totally blocking the view. The wind seemed to be blowing from the east, so we were driving into the storm. Every few minutes, a gust would blow a large sheet of snow from the road onto the windshield. I couldn't slow down or I would lose momentum and be stuck. Thankfully, the wipers were doing their job.

The road had about six inches of new snow and we had to try and stay in the one track someone had made just ahead of us. Snow was still falling heavily. If we strayed from the previous track, the car would swerve, and we would have to fight to keep control. I worried about being stranded since neither one of us handles cold that well any more. I sure didn't want to be stuck there overnight.

We met several cars coming the other way and had to be sure we were on our side of the road. The main track, of course, was a bit in the center of the roadway, as we tend to do when we can't see the edge of the road. I could see flashing lights ahead in the oncoming lane and hoped there had not been an accident. It turned out to be a tow truck helping someone who had been pulling a loaded snow-mobile trailer. The whiteout conditions must have been too serious even for snowmobilers.

My car was handling nicely, and I was delighted to have made it this far. What a joy to be alive and able to cope with what nature was throwing at us. We were coming up to the turn off, so I honked, hoping Ray could hear me and let me go ahead since that was the plan. I guess he thought I wanted him to go first to break the trail for me. It was a surprise to learn later that we can't hear a car honk when the wipers are on full speed.

Finally, we arrived at our turn off and noticed that conditions were better on our tree-lined drive. The snow was deep but wasn't blowing so we had better viability. I stayed far enough back in case he didn't make it all the way up the hill and had to back down. Ray's truck made the hill without incident, so I drove on up with my all-wheel drive.

The adventure wasn't over yet since we had to unload the groceries and then move my car. Earlier that week, we had turned the plowing over to Phil. Since Phil would be out to plow either that afternoon or the next morning, I had to move my car over to a tight space by the propane tank. The car was pulled in as far as I could go into the snow drift to allow space for the plow to get past. I decided to dig out my handy windshield cover since snow was still falling. The parking spot was so tight that I couldn't walk around the front of the car, but I had at least covered the windshield on the driver's side.

Coming around the front of the car, I stumbled on something hard under the snow and fell into about three feet of the soft fluffy stuff. I had nothing to grab ahold of and the snow was too soft to get a grip, so I had to crawl on my knees over to the door of the car, so I could pull myself up by the handle. By the time I got to the house, Ray was standing at the door wondering what had taken so long. What a nice feeling to know that he was there and that I was loved.

Sometimes, Ray and I try to visualize how life would be if we moved to town. Maybe we could find a townhouse where someone else mows the grass and takes care of repairs. But then, we would only have a wall between us and some others like us who have to turn our music or the TV up a little louder so we can hear it. Also, we have grown used to life without the sound of sirens and traffic or street lights at night to keep us awake.

We know living here in the woods is not going to get any easier as we grow older. I had to have surgery on my varicose veins in the spring of 2018, and I still need new knees. Ray still needs a shoulder replacement. So, we were happy to learn of a young fellow who wanted to earn a little extra money mowing grass. It was just in the nick of time. We know we will have to hire more and more help as the years go by. But our roots have taken hold in this rocky soil and we can't imagine a life quite this enjoyable anywhere else.

EPILOGUE
A Dream Come True

The canoe glided smoothly through the quiet waters as the pair talked and laughed softly to themselves. They were as comfortable with their craft as they were with each other as they paddled leisurely, obviously enjoying their surroundings. The sun was unseasonably warm and reflected off the cold lake water. A solitary loon was skirting the opposite shore and the only sound was the slow rhythmic dip of the canoe's paddles as the couple enjoyed their afternoon outing.

The man sat in the stern and easily guided the canoe as his companion paddled from the bow, pulling the canoe through the water with strong steady strokes. Her strength and energy might have been surprising to those who judged her by her great-grandmother status. Her thoughts were filled with the richest of memories and even thoughts about a future road trip. His once dark curly hair was totally white now. But he had a sparkle in his pale blue eyes, and his lips were curved into that slightly crooked smile that she had come to love.

Green branches brightened up the splintery gray trunks of cedar trees and the mottled trunks of the red and white pines. Rocks along the shore were dappled with lichen and sunlight danced over the ripples on the lake. It was a moment to savor. A time to be thankful.

Barely discernible through the trees were glimpses of a log cabin. The house rose nearly to the tops of the tall pines that circled it, but it was built back far enough from the lake to blend unobtrusively into the surroundings.

The woman pointed to the cabin. "How would you like to live in a place like that?"

He smiled as she turned around to watch his face. "That would be a dream come true, wouldn't it?" he said.

She returned his smile and they paddled over to the shore, steadied the canoe for each other, and carefully disembarked. Then they began the long climb to their cabin on the hill.

ABOUT THE AUTHORS

ROSE THIELBAR grew up on a farm in Illinois so transitioning to life in the Northwoods was a natural progression. She considers watching animal (and human) behavior endlessly fascinating. She also enjoys a good road trip with her husband to explore new and beautiful places. Her favorite thing is walking along the shore of a rushing stream. She thrives on books to read, gardens to tend and annual visits from children and grandchildren. Work experiences were as a Tele-typist, a bookkeeper, an income tax preparer, and a newspaper writer. She wrote five different monthly newsletters through the years, just for the fun of it.

RAY THIELBAR was an Illinois River town boy, raised by a mom who was musical and a dad with a "can-do" ability. He married his high school sweetheart, attended Eureka College and Moody Bible Institute and finally decided on a career path with Caterpillar Tractor Co. as a Metallurgist. Scaling the ladder of responsibility included various levels of management and five years in Brazil. With his wife, Rose, they raised a family of three great kids who also share an appreciation for outdoor activities, as well as a wide variety of other interests. In 2018, Ray received the *Music & Drama Community Service to the Arts Award* for his contributions of music, and of art, by way of the many hand carved wooden signs which he made for the Bear and Wolf centers and various businesses in Ely. Perhaps, his greatest contribution was his 25 years of leadership in planning the annual community Thanksgathering program.

Electric Moon Publishing, LLC is an author-friendly, custom publishing place.
EMoon collaborates with indie authors, ministries, organizations, and businesses in writing,
editing, custom covers, specialty layouts, print, distribution, and marketing.

Visit us at www.emoonpublishing.com
or contact us directly at info@emoonpublishing.com.

43448994R00212

Made in the USA
Middletown, DE
25 April 2019